The Story of
GUILDFORD

Frozen River Wey, 1895.
Reproduced by permission of Surrey History Centre.

The Story of
GUILDFORD

MARION FIELD

Phillimore

2011

Published by
PHILLIMORE & CO. LTD
Healey House, Andover, Hampshire

© Marion Field, 2011

ISBN 978-1-86077-673-1

Printed and bound in Malta

Manufacturing managed by
Jellyfish Solutions Ltd

Contents

List of Illustrations

Frontispiece: Frozen River Wey, 1895.

Acknowledgements

Dr Mary Alexander; the *Angel*; Mr and Mrs Bowerman; Ms Mary Buylla; Cathedral Archives (figs 67, 90, 92-3, 95-101, 103-6); the Rev. Andrew Cowie; Mrs Meriel Forshaw; Guildford Museum; Ms Hannah Jeffery, Archivist at Surrey Archaeological Society; Mrs Elizabeth North, Archivist at Guildford Cathedral; Mrs Lyndsay Piper; Julian Pooley, Archivist at Surrey History Centre; Mr Tony Richmond, Master of Abbot's Hospital (fig. 34); Ms Maureen Shettle, Archivist at University of Surrey; Mr Gregory Scholfield; Surrey Archaeological Society Archives (figs 3-8, 9-12, 17-18, 23-6, 31, 39-40, 45-6, 49-51, 61, 66, 69, 89, 110); Surrey History Centre (figs 13-14, 16, 19-21, 27, 32-3, 43-4, 47-8, 52-8, 60, 62, 70-9, 82-4, 87-8, 111-13); Woking Library; Yvonne Arnaud box office; Laura Butler at the Yvonne Arnaud Theatre (fig. 81). The remaining illustrations (figs 1-2, 15, 22, 28-30, 35-6, 37-8, 41-2, 43-4, 59, 63-5, 68, 80, 85-6, 91, 94, 102, 107-10, 114-15) are the property of the author.

One

Origins – The Anglo-Saxons

Guildford, the county town of Surrey, has been important since Saxon times. It has provided a residence for royalty and many famous men and women, and has been the setting for several important historical events. Its landscape is impressive in itself: Guildford grew up in a gap in a long range of beautiful chalk hills created centuries ago when the River Wey forced its way through the North Downs towards the larger River Thames. The original Saxon village was probably built on the western bank of the river, and the development of a ford here presumably explains the second syllable of the town's name, originally Gyldeforda. It is possible that a wooden bridge was constructed here, but no timber has ever been found to support this; however, excavations have discovered timber reinforcements from a medieval wharf. The first syllable of the settlement's name is not so easily attributed, as guilds did not appear until much later: the area had a name long before they came into being. Perhaps 'Guild' is a corruption of golden: the *Oxford Dictionary of Place Names* suggests that the area became the Golden Ford because of the number of yellow marsh marigolds that litter the banks of the river. Another suggestion is that gold refers to the colour of the sands on the riverbank or on the riverbed. There has also been a suggestion that the river may at one time have been called Guilon or Gil.[1]

It is likely that there were Bronze and Iron Age settlements in St Catherine's, which lies to the south of Guildford. A possible place where the Saxons might have worshipped is the top of St Catherine's Hill, on which stand the ruins of a chapel built in the 14th century. Another site for pagan worship might have been the spring at the bottom of Ferry Lane; this was reputed to have healing properties. Tradition has hinted that the Saxon King Ethelred established a

1   *Site of Saxon cemetery.*

palace on the site where the Normans later built a castle, but there is little evidence for this.

There appears to be no evidence of Roman occupation in the area, although they built villas elsewhere in Surrey, preferring in general to settle further east. The first settlers for whom there is definite evidence are the Anglo-Saxons at the beginning of the sixth century. They were migrants from north-western Europe, who were pagan and worshipped many gods. They built a number of rectangular wooden huts on the west bank of the ford, although later they moved the settlement to the east bank, where a watch tower was built.

In 1929 archaeologists excavating the Mount, on the western slope of the Downs, made an exciting discovery: 35 skeletons from the sixth century, indicating that this was a Saxon cemetery as their dead were buried away from the main settlement. As the Saxons believed that items used in life were still needed after death, bodies were buried alongside spears, knives, pots and even glass beakers. Necklaces and brooches were also found, suggesting that the corpses were fully clothed: the brooches would have been used to fasten their clothing.

During the following century missionaries from Winchester were sent to convert the heathen. They appear to have succeeded, as artefacts were no longer buried with the deceased. It is likely that a small wooden church was built on the site of the present St Mary's Church, around the earlier watch-tower – so the Saxon tower is Guildford's oldest building.[2]

2   *Saxon Tower on St Mary's Church.*

It was in the ninth century that Gyldeforda first appears in a written record: in about 880 Alfred the Great left his 'royal residence' at Gyldeforda to his nephew, Aethelward. There is no archaeological evidence of a castle at this time but there is a possibility that one had been built on the Mount, which would have provided a natural defence. The present castle, of which only ruins remain, was probably built soon after the Normans appeared.

It was probably about the beginning of the 10th century that the town was enlarged.[3] Never having been a Roman settlement, there were no walls; the Saxons dug ditches to mark the town's boundaries. These would have stretched from the Friary area along North Street and around St Mary's; today's North Street would have been the site of the North Ditch. The land around the High Street was thus enclosed, with long narrow strips of land on either side of it on which houses were built. It is possible that, as a defence measure, the ford was replaced with a wooden bridge.

During the 970s Guildford became an important commercial centre. This was mainly because a royal mint was set up here by King Edward, giving the town the status of a borough. The earliest coins, produced during his reign, were silver pennies engraved with the name Dunstan. Some sources suggest that this might have been the St Dunstan who was made Archbishop of Canterbury in 960. St Dunstan was born near Glastonbury in the early 10th century to a Wessex nobleman. He was educated at Glastonbury Abbey and took holy orders in 943. After that he lived simply in a small cell near the abbey where, as well as leading a life of devotion, he also honed his practical metalworking skills – which explains why he later became the patron saint of metalworkers. But Dunstan was not destined to remain devoted to this simple life. The king, Edmund, summoned him to court to act as his priest and advisor, and he continued in this role with Edmund's successors. He still kept his interest in his metalworking, however; there is even a tradition that he designed the crown for King Edgar's coronation in 959. When Edgar died in 975, his son Edward became king, at the tender age of 12, and Dunstan was able to guide and help the young king in this demanding role. He travelled around the kingdom with his sovereign and is said to have visited Guildford on several occasions.[4]

However, it seems more likely that the Dunstan whose name appears on the coins was a man with the same name – the 'moneyer' or master of the Guildford Mint. The shortened name of the town also appeared on the coins. Over the years this varied, becoming Gyld, Gyl or even the very brief Gy. The coins that were produced later under other moneyers, such as Dunglild and Leopold, were not of such fine craftsmanship as the early ones that bore Dunstan's name.[5]

3   *A coin, c.12th-century.*

The royal mint in Guildford continued to flourish for many years. During the reign of Edward the Confessor, who ascended the throne in 1042, a number of new coins were struck. Some were known as sovereigns, and these showed the king seated on a chair of state. Others depicted the king's face alone. On the reverse of all these coins were the arms of Edward the Confessor – a blue shield bearing a cross 'moline'.[6]

Guildford was an important staging-post between Winchester and London. At this time, and until after the Norman Conquest, Winchester was the capital of England, while London was already the country's most important trading centre. Guildford's pivotal role at this time led to a notorious incident in 1036, which the town would prefer to forget: an appalling massacre, on an unknown site, related to the friction between Vikings and Saxons. There is enough documentary and archaeological evidence to ascertain the main facts, even if the various accounts vary in detail.

At the start of the 11th century, after a comparatively peaceful period, the Vikings from Norway, under Canute, raided the country and defeated the Saxon king, Ethelred the Unready, at the Battle of Assandun in Essex. Canute took possession of Mercia and Northumbria, and when Ethelred died in 1016 Canute became king of all England. To make his position more secure he married Emma of Normandy, Ethelred's widow, and exiled her two sons, Alfred and Edward, to Normandy. When Canute died in 1035 his son, Harold, took over the throne, but it is likely that Emma wanted her sons to be restored to their rightful heritage. She had retired to Winchester where the people regarded her with affection,[7] and she lived as a devout widow, filling her days with good works. Her two sons remained in Normandy but it was becoming increasingly dangerous for them. Their guardian, the Duke of Normandy, had recently died on a pilgrimage to the Holy Land, so they were without his valuable protection. Perhaps because they felt threatened in Normandy, they decided to visit their mother in England. However, there is a suggestion that they fell into a trap – that Earl Godwin, who was the king's representative in Guildford, forged a letter from Emma asking her sons to visit. Whatever the reason for their journey, according to the *Anglo-Saxon Chronicle** they travelled to Winchester

---

*   The *Anglo-Saxon Chronicle* was compiled in A.D. 890 during the reign of Alfred the Great. It was distributed around the country and local scribes updated events in Old English, the language that had developed from a combination of Germanic and Nordic languages and the local Saxon.

and met their mother. The *Chronicle* suggests that the two had merely come to visit their mother, but Florence (or Florentius) of Worcester (d. 1118), an English monk who wrote an account of the incident a century later, suggests that Alfred, the younger son, 'was hastening towards London to a parley with King Harold'. So another possibility is that while in Winchester Emma's sons received a letter from King Harold inviting the young men to travel to London to join his court.

Emma was a very intelligent woman, and she did not trust Harold. She and many others in the country felt that it was Edward, her elder son, who was the rightful heir to the throne and not the Viking Harold – who probably felt threatened by Ethelred's sons. Wary of a trap, Emma compromised. She kept Edward with her at Winchester and sent her younger son, Alfred, to London with a troop of 600 Norman soldiers. He was met at a point between Farnham and Guildford by Earl Godwin. Godwin was a clever, unscrupulous man who had high ambitions. Although a Saxon, he had been loyal to Canute, who had rewarded him by creating him Earl of Wessex, one of the three great earldoms in the country. This stretched across the south of England from Cornwall to Kent, so Guildford came within his jurisdiction. Godwin married Canute's sister-in-law, Gytha, and after Canute's death his loyalties remained with Canute's son, Harold. However, it has been suggested that during the journey to Guildford Godwin offered Alfred his allegiance to the Saxon cause, on condition that Alfred married his daughter, Editha. Alfred angrily refused, and thus perhaps sealed his fate. Or had Harold already instructed Godwin to dispose of one if not both of the Saxon claimants to the throne?

Whatever the reason for the journey, there is no doubt about what followed. Godwin escorted the prince and his retinue to Guildford, where they were to rest before continuing their journey. The soldiers were divided into small groups and billeted in various places around the town. The prince and those close to him were entertained to a lavish feast before retiring to sleep – but they were not allowed to sleep for long. In the middle of the night they were woken up, dragged from their beds and 'loaded with chains and gives'. Early the next morning they were led into the street and slaughtered with the most horrendous brutality. One in every group of 10 men was spared, and forced to witness the appalling massacre of his colleagues. Prince Alfred was not killed immediately, but captured and taken to the monastery of Ely. Here he was tortured and blinded, and eventually died from his injuries.

Florence of Worcester blamed Godwin alone for the massacre of nearly 600 men on that dreadful day, but a contemporary account, the *Enconium Emma Retinae*, commissioned by Alfred's mother, Emma, has a different view.

This document was written in 1041-2 by a monk from St-Bertin in St-Omer, Flanders, as a propaganda exercise, and informs the reader that 'the course of this book is devoted entirely to the praise of Queen Emma'. Emma was in no doubt that Godwin was acting under orders from King Harold, which in her eyes made the king entirely to blame for the massacre. The anonymous writer had no qualms about distorting the truth to achieve his ends, and so perhaps his statements should not be taken too seriously, but his account of the massacre is supported by other evidence.

Whoever was responsible, both accounts speak of the barbarity shown to the soldiers. The *Enconium Emma Retinae* states: 'They were all disarmed and delivered with their hands bound behind their backs, to most vicious executioners who were ordered to spare not man ... [and they] butchered the innocent heroes with blows from their spears, bound as though they were swine.'[8]

The cemetery on the Mount used earlier as a Saxon burial ground was now used to bury the victims of this massacre. The earlier burials had been performed with reverence and order, but the many skeletons found on top were flung into the ground with no respect. Many had their hands tied behind their backs and had been brutally speared or hacked. This physical evidence, uncovered in 1929, supports the documentary evidence of a massacre carried out a thousand years before.

When King Harold died in 1040 the country was in turmoil for two years, as the kingdoms into which the country was divided competed against each other. No doubt seizing the main chance, Godwin realised that the wise thing to do would be to support Edward, Emma's elder son, in his claim to the throne. The Saxons considered him the rightful king and there was no obvious Viking heir. Godwin, accepting the inevitable, therefore switched sides and was probably instrumental in putting Edward, who became known as 'the Confessor', on the throne, thereby uniting the various kingdoms. Edward was crowned in 1042, so Emma had her wish and the Saxons were at last restored to the English throne.

Godwin consolidated his position at Edward's court by persuading the king to marry his daughter, Edith, in 1045. However, Edward did not like his father-in-law and had not forgiven him for the murder of his brother, Alfred. Neither was he impressed with his new wife, and tradition suggests that the marriage was never consummated. The fact that Edward had no children gives credence to this view. While Edward's father had been Saxon, his mother was of Norman stock, and he had spent his formative years from 1013 to 1041 in exile in Normandy. When he came to the throne he placed a number of Normans in high office, often overriding Earl Godwin's choice of candidates. In 1051 he appointed Robert, Abbot of Jumièges, as Archbishop of Canterbury, passing over Godwin's candidate to Godwin's chagrin. The same year Edward made two other important decisions. Tired of his unsatisfactory marriage, he sent Edith to a nunnery at Wherwell. Then, to ensure that Earl Godwin's line would not succeed to the throne, he nominated his relative, William of Normandy, as heir to the English throne. The English nobles, including Godwin and his family, swore to accept this – and Edward took some of Godwin's family hostage to ensure their allegiance.

Godwin died in 1053, and his son Harold succeeded him as earl. The Godwins continued to be a thorn in Edward's side. To make sure that the new earl would not cause problems, the king sent him to Normandy to greet William, his heir. There, Harold swore publicly, on oath, that he would support William's claim to the English throne. He paid homage to the duke and thus became his vassal. To break such an oath would have been regarded at this time as a heinous sin.

When on 5 January 1066 Edward died at Westminster he left no male heir. Harold broke his oath and seized the throne in a *coup d'état*. Immediately afterwards Halley's comet blazed in the sky for a week. This event was said to foretell doom, but Harold ignored it. No doubt William of Normandy saw it as a good omen for his invasion. He was furious that Harold had seized the throne after swearing an oath of allegiance to him only two years earlier, and he knew that he had the support of much of Europe, including that of the pope.

Why Harold seized the throne in such a hurry and, by so doing, committed perjury – one of the worst sins – is not completely clear, but it has been suggested that Edward named Harold as his successor on his deathbed. Whatever the reason, Harold was hurriedly crowned on 6 January 1066, on the same day that his predecessor was being buried. Perhaps he suspected that William was on his way to claim the throne. Events were to unfold that meant he was unable to enjoy his new office for long.[9]

The Vikings were still convinced that they were entitled to the throne, and the King of Norway, Harald Hardrada, was determined to wrest the throne from the upstart Saxon. In September 1066 he assembled a large fleet and sailed up the Humber and the Ouse to land in York. But the Saxons were prepared. Just outside the city the Vikings were confronted by Edwin, Earl of Mercia, and Morcar, Earl of Northumbria, with their armies. In a bloody battle on 20 September the Saxons were defeated and the King of Norway continued on his way. But his claim to the English throne was doomed to failure. Seven miles from York, at Stamford Bridge, he met Harold with his army. On Monday 25 September a bloody battle took place, and Harald Hardrada, described as the last heroic figure of the Viking age, was slain; Harold, King of England, was triumphant. He celebrated his victory with a feast at York, and tradition suggests that it was during this feast that he received the unwelcome news that William, Duke of Normandy, had sailed across the English Channel and landed with his army on the south coast of England. To show his support, Pope Alexander II had sent William a banner under which to march.

Harold's celebrations were curtailed, and he prepared to face his rival. For 13 days his weary army marched south to Hastings, where the Normans had set up their camp. He arrived on the evening of 13 October and pitched camp about seven miles away from the Normans. The following morning the trumpets signalled the start of one of the most famous battles in history. As the armies engaged, the Normans released arrows and the Saxons retaliated by hurling spears, axes and stones at their enemy. But the Normans were better trained and had horses and swords. They were also fresher, as Harold's army was exhausted by the battle at Stamford Bridge and their long march south. Tired and dispirited, the Saxons were no match for the superior archery and cavalry of the Normans. Harold's brothers, Gyrth and Leofwine, were both slain, and by the evening the Saxons knew they had been defeated. The final blow came when Harold himself was, according to the Bayeux Tapestry, struck in the eye by a Norman arrow and killed. William claimed victory and was crowned king at Westminster Abbey on Christmas Day 1066. So the year of 1066 saw a coronation at its beginning and another at its end.

Two

The Normans and Medieval Guildford

After William had established his right to the throne it was necessary for him to demonstrate his authority to his Saxon subjects. He did this by sending his knights around the country to subjugate the inhabitants, by whatever means they chose. Those who resisted suffered severely; towns were ransacked and some were even completely destroyed. William made it clear that he would brook no insubordination. Fortunately Guildford did not suffer the same fate as its neighbour Shalford, which went up in flames. One reason for Guildford being spared was probably its excellent strategic position, not only between Winchester and London but also connected to the coast by an ancient track.

William wanted to know everything about the country that now came under his jurisdiction. In particular he wanted to know how much it was worth, and therefore how much money he could hope to extract from its citizens. To this end he conducted the first survey of its kind since the days of the Roman empire. He sent a group of royal officers, known as 'legati', to each county, where they held a public assembly to which were summoned representatives of each town. Questions were prepared and the answers were carefully noted. More detailed than an ordinary census, it recorded the land owned by various manorial lords, the number of those employed in each manor, the extent of cultivated land and even the number and type of livestock. It took William's commissioners eight months to complete this, and they compiled two million words – surely the most comprehensive survey of England before or since. Finished in 1086, it acquired the name Domesday – as the people regarded it as 'the last trump of doom from which there was no appeal'.[1]

Originally the results of the returns were divided into hundreds. A county was divided into several hundreds, each of which had its own assembly of village representatives and notables.[2] Later the contents of the survey had to be reorganised into the smaller fiefs that were held by tenants. At the time Domesday was compiled Guildford was in the manor or hundred of Woking, but it was considered important enough to have its own entry: 'In Gildeford King William has 75 *hagae* in which live 175 tenants. TRE it rendered £18. 3d.; now it is worth £30 and yet it renders £32.'[3] The Latin word *hagae* probably came from the Saxon word for hedge, suggesting some type of enclosure. It has also been translated as close – a term that could be applied to an enclosure of several houses.[4] TRE is the abbreviation for *tempora regis Eduardis*, or 'during the reign of Edward the Confessor', at which time it was assumed that everything had been done correctly and legally. The commissioners found that 'Ranulf the clerk has 3 closes in which 6 men dwell ... and would receive the tax from them unless a general tax [geld] was levied on the town'.[5] The Ranulf referred to, according to Manning,[6] was 'Ranulph Flambard who held the Church of Godalming at this time of the king; and these tenements were part of it'. Interestingly there is no record in the Domesday Book of a church or a mill in Guildford.

William planned to build a castle from which he could dominate the town and intimidate his resentful subjects. The Normans had invented these fortified buildings as a base to garrison the soldiers who controlled towns. Many had

4   *Guildford Castle.*

5 *The north-west view of Guildford Castle, 1737. Reproduced from an old print drawn and engraved by Samuel and Nathaniel Buck, and dedicated to the Rt Hon. Arthur Onslow, Speaker of the House of Commons.*

been built on the continent but there were none in England. Guildford was an ideal location, and building probably started soon after 1066; however, the actual date is not known. The builders started by digging a circular ditch, and they flung the displaced earth into the centre to form a large mound. This was known as a motte, and upon it a strong tower was later erected. Originally this may have been surrounded by a timber palisade. The tower, dominating the town, would have been used only as a lookout. There would have been a

6 *Guildford Castle.*

7 *The undercroft under the* Angel Inn.

bridge over the ditch from the motte for access to the bailey, the rectangular area surrounding the motte. This probably consisted of five to six acres and was divided into an inner bailey and an outer bailey. The outer area was used for stabling horses and grazing livestock, while the buildings in the inner bailey would have been the king's residence when he was in the area, during his travels around the kingdom in order to consolidate his position.

During the next few years Guildford saw little military action and the castle gradually ceased to be a military stronghold, becoming more of a palace than a fortress. There was more building on the site, although it is not known when this started.

By the beginning of the 12th century Guildford had become a wealthy town. It owed its prosperity to the wool trade introduced into the west of Surrey by the Cistercian monks who founded Waverley Abbey, near Farnham, in 1128. Guildford specialised in producing great quantities of a cloth known as kersey, which was very coarse. There was plenty of rich pasture for the sheep on the surrounding downs. After sheep were shorn, their fleeces were spun into yarn, and this was woven into cloth. Some of this was sent to Guildford and to other towns for the finishing processes. The first of these was fulling, where the cloth was placed in a tub of water and pummelled to clean and degrease it, producing a smooth nap. An important deposit of Fuller's earth, which was used for cleaning the wool, was found not far from Guildford, and the River Wey provided clean water for fulling. Following the fulling process, the cloth was dyed, often with woad to produce the popular blue cloth. This was then hooked to racks so that it would dry evenly. When dry, the nap was brushed and sheared until the surface was smooth. Guildford was fortunate in having suitable conditions for the growing of teasels, which are rather like thistles; they were used for teasing the nap. Because the teasel crop was so large, they were even sold to other wool-growing areas. After teasing was complete, the wool was ready for sale.[7]

Possibly associated with the wool trade was the construction in Guildford during the late 13th century of a number of undercrofts. These stone-vaulted cellars served as shops, and an example still survives today underneath the *Angel Hotel*.[8]

8 *The undercroft under the* Angel Inn.

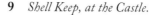

9   *Shell Keep, at the Castle.*

10   *The King's Chamber in the Castle.*

It was perhaps early in the 12th century that a chalk shell-keep was built at the castle, encircling the top of the motte. Later in the same century a stone tower keep replaced the original one, and this is one of the few parts of the castle that still survive. There is little documentary evidence of the early history of the castle; the earliest reference to it is in 1173-4, when the castle walls were strengthened on the orders of King Henry II. In 1173 there had been an attempt to depose the king and place his young son on the throne, and this strengthening of the castle's defences was apparently successful in helping to put down the young king's rebellion.

The castle continued to be used by successive kings, and in the 12th century additions were made to make it more comfortable. Within the bailey a great hall was built, as the king and his retinue were frequent visitors. Meals were prepared in the nearby kitchen and served in

11   *Interior of the keep.*

the hall, which also provided sleeping quarters: there was little privacy for either the royal visitor or his family and followers.

Another area visited by the monarch was Stag Hill, on the north side of the Hog's Back. This vast green space was populated only by deer, which gave it its name. Unlike St Catherine's on the south side, which had probably boasted a religious shrine of some sort for centuries, no building took place on this site until the 20th century. In 1155 Henry II enclosed it, making it into a royal park where he and his successors would enjoy hunting stags.

Another addition to Guildford, in 1200, was a stone bridge built across the ancient ford by the monks of Waverly Abbey. This survived until the beginning of the 20th century.

In 1995 archaeologists discovered the remains of an interesting stone room underneath a shop in the High Street. While its origin is debatable, many historians believe it was once a synagogue. If so, it was probably constructed in about 1180 as part of a house. There was a stone bench around the walls of the 10ft-square room, and a 12th-century coin was found in a crack in this bench. One of the two doorways was approached by a flight of steps, and originally there might have been a number of colonnaded recesses. The floors would have been of wood and tile, and the whole area would have been richly decorated in red, black and indigo. The latter was an expensive pigment from the Orient, suggesting that the owner of the house was a wealthy man. The synagogue, if such it was, was demolished in about 1290. As this was the time that the Jews were expelled from England, this gives some credence to the possibility that the construction was indeed a synagogue.

So there were certainly Jews in Guildford during the 12th and 13th centuries, although Guildford was not one of the towns in which they were officially permitted to live. Many of them were wealthy, and because Henry II needed money to fund a crusade he levied a tallage on them in 1187 – the 'fourth part of their goods and chattels towards the expense of a crusade to Palestine'.[9] Tallage was a land tax that had been introduced into England by the Normans and became an important source of royal revenue. During the 12th and 13th centuries it was frequently levied on the Jews. Two years later, in 1189, Henry's son Richard I also levied the 'Saladin tallage' on the Jews to help fund the Third Crusade. Isaac, the son of a Guildford rabbi, was fined the vast sum of £200 for refusing to pay it, but was permitted to pay the fine in instalments: '£100 was to be paid on the Sunday when Laetare Jerusalem was sung, and the other at the rate of £30 a year till the debt was liquidated, £15 being payable at Michaelmas, and £15 at Easter'.[10] Richard I's brother, King John, also tallaged the Jews to the value of about £40,000, in 1210.

King John visited Guildford 19 times. In 1199 he celebrated Christmas in the town in luxurious style, and robed his followers in spectacular new garments. Legend suggests that he was extremely annoyed to be outshone in splendour by a priest – possibly the Archbishop of Canterbury. A ballad of the time, 'King John and the Abbot', took up the story and embroidered it for posterity. Towards the end of John's brief reign he passed through the town several times, perhaps to get away from his barons who were becoming increasingly disillusioned with their unsatisfactory king. He was aware that Guildford was a wealthy town, and on 15 June 1213 he issued a writ to the Approved Men of Guildford 'commanding them to provide with arms and horses twenty men of the better sort within their Vill to be ready to go beyond the seas on the King's service whensoever he should call them forth'.[11] Presumably he was thinking of a crusade.

On Monday 15 June 1215 they barons met King John near Windsor, in Runnymede meadow beside the Thames. Here they forced him to sign the *Magna Carta*. Because of the changing boundaries of the river over the centuries, it is not possible today to pinpoint the exact place where the signing of this historic document took place. It dealt with a number of issues and reiterated the rights of the Church, the barons and all free citizens. The most important clause confirmed the right to justice for all and freedom from unwarranted imprisonment. It also condemned the use of tallage, but this continued to be levied until it was finally abolished by Edward III in 1340. John ignored the promises he had made, and continued on his downward spiral.

The king's last visit to Guildford was in April 1216. Shortly after this the barons, losing patience with him, summoned help from King Louis of France, who sent his son, the Dauphin, across the Channel. He proceeded to Guildford and took up residence in the castle, where his followers did a great deal of damage. John died soon afterwards, leaving his nine-year-old son Henry to ascend a very fragile throne in October 1216. Fortunately he had some very capable deputies to govern the country until he came of age. They expelled the French invaders and crushed any remaining adherents of his father.

Henry III was very attached to Guildford, and in 1251 he set up three mills in the area – a corn mill, a malt mill and one of the newly invented fulling mills. This was a machine where water-wheels powered large wooden mallets which hammered the wool to clean it. Sir Richard Testard, whose ancestors had been granted land by William the Conqueror, was not happy that the king had set up new mills in competition with the one he ran on the opposite side of the river. The fulling mills certainly contributed to the continuing success of the wool trade, but later they caused flooding and damaged the other mills, so they were closed down in 1267. There was also another mill, owned by the Manor of Artington, near St Nicolas's Church.

By the end of the 13th century the de la Poyle family had acquired the Testard land, and in 1295 Walter de la Poyle paid 2s. 'to have a watercourse at his mill'. By the end of the 14th century Arlington Mill also possessed a fulling mill, and John Atte Lee, the fuller, set up his drying racks or tenter frames in Mill Mead, where horses had previously grazed. The name Millmead still survives for this area.

As the cloth trade increased, the masters of the smaller trade guilds organised themselves into a guild merchant, similar to groups that had been in operation on the Continent for some time. The idea of guilds, groups bonded together to further a particular craft or trade, may have its roots in Roman times, but by the Middle Ages most of the Roman fraternities had disappeared. They began to surface again in the 11th century when associations of groups or crafts were formed. They were often founded by craftsmen who were masters in their fields – textile workers, masons, carpenters and others – and they controlled the secrets of their trade. The master was an expert and would have undergone a long period of training. Members of the guild took an oath to serve their town and the king.[12]

However, the guilds were not always able to prevent fraud, even when they were aware of it. Towards the end of the 14th century one method of defrauding customers was by artificially stretching the cloth while it was still wet. When dry, the cloth would appear longer than it actually was, but if it became wet it would shrink to its correct length. To prevent the fraud, some manufacturers attached lead seals to their cloth to identify it. These were a form of maker's mark and a guarantee of quality. After the cloth was sold, they were removed. They became a form of currency, and were often used to represent the cloth when it was sold or purchased.[13] The practice of stretching continued, however, and in 1391 even Parliament was concerned that Guildford's reputation as an honest wool-trading town was being ruined by 'unscrupulous clothiers' who followed this practice. Despite attempts to stop it, it continued for the next 300 years, although some customers returned stretched cloth, which could then be sold 'at no market'. It has been suggested that this dishonesty contributed to the decline of the wool trade in Guildford.

The guilds became a powerful group in Guildford, and acquired total control over the town and its citizens. They even presided over their own court. The head of the merchant guild was known as the seneschal. He was

12   *Details of Queen Eleanor's boudoir from 1974 excavations.*

an officer of the king's household and had duties to his sovereign as well as to the town. It was a distinct advantage for the town to have an important figure in place who had links both to court and Parliament. There are records of seneschals from 1362 to 1378, but from then until 1413 the records have been lost. The term mayor was probably used some time after 1366, when Guildford acquired the right to collect fees that were due to the king.

During his long reign of 50 years Henry III visited Guildford over 100 times. Realising its growing potential for trade, he granted the borough its first charter in January 1257. This merchants' charter freed the 'good men of Guildford' from the threat of arrest for other people's debts. Eight months after granting this charter Henry also gave the town the honour of holding the county court and assizes. It thus became the county town of Surrey, and had the right to select two members of Parliament.

As he visited the town so often, Henry determined to make the castle a more appropriate place for the sovereign to stay. In spite of the damage caused by the Dauphin's men, the structure of the building was sound. Henry proceeded to transform it into a luxurious palace. Privacy had become more important, and private apartments were created for the king, his family and important members of the court. Henry's private chamber was panelled with wood, and the ceiling was decorated with a moon and stars. Nearby was the king's private chapel. The young Prince Edward had his own chamber, and a new 'wardrobe' was provided for Queen Eleanor. Glass, both plain and coloured, was used in the apartments and in the great hall. The walls of the latter were decorated with murals painted by an Italian, William the Florentine, who had been commissioned by the king to oversee the building works. However, Henry had no intention of paying for all this work himself. He

ordered the Sheriff of Surrey to see to the repairs of the pictures in the great
hall without delay; and in his great chamber, at the head of the bed, was to
be painted a curtain on the white wall. The tablets and frontal of the altar of
the great chapel to be finished agreeably to the design of William of Florence,
the painter, the county to bear the expense of these improvements.

The queen's kitchen garden was also 'to be repaired and set in order'.[14]
Queen Eleanor was obviously a keen gardener and interested in design. She
introduced colonnaded gardens and tiled pavements to the area.

Henry's improvements extended to St Mary's Church in Quarry Street.
As previously noted, there had probably been a wooden church on the site
since soon after Christianity came to Guildford, although there is no record
of it in the Domesday Book. It was rebuilt in stone either by the Saxons or
during the early Norman period, and in the 12th century it was enlarged by
the canons of Merton Priory, who had been given the church in about 1120
by the king. More improvements followed when side aisles were added to
the nave. During the 1250s these aisles were extended and Biblical scenes
were painted in the side chapels, possibly by William the Florentine.

In 1266 there was a rebellion against Henry by Simon de Montfort. Prince
Edward captured one of the rebels, Adam de Gurdon, and incarcerated him
in Guildford Castle before his execution. However, Edward's wife, Eleanor
of Castile, pleaded for the rebel's life, and Edward granted her wish.

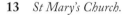 **13**   *St Mary's Church.*

 *Reproduced by permission of Surrey History Centre.*

14 & 16 reproduced by permission of Surrey History Centre.

14   *St Mary's Church.*

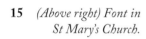

15   *(Above right) Font in St Mary's Church.*

16   *Interior of St Mary's Church.*

When Henry III died in 1272 his widow, Eleanor of Provence, gained control of Guildford, as it had been one of the towns included in her dowry. Three years later she expelled the Jews from all her towns, including Guildford. The new king, Edward I, was not as attached to Guildford as his father had been. Royal visits to the borough decreased in frequency, and the new king had no money to spend on much-needed maintenance for the castle. In 1274 tragedy struck the king and his wife, Eleanor of Castile, when their six-year-old son, Henry, who had been ill for some time, died in Guildford. The parents were heartbroken, and so was the boy's grandmother, Eleanor of Provence, who had looked after the little boy for two years while his parents had been away. She was determined that he would not be forgotten, and so decided to found a Dominican friary in his memory. Her daughter-in-law, the boy's mother, was the nursing mother of the Dominican friars, and she may have influenced her mother-in-law. The Dominicans were a preaching order, and as they believed that they could save souls by preaching they always settled in towns. As they were poor, they lived by begging alms from the townspeople. Guildford was an ideal place for a Dominican friary.

It is possible that a small order of the Friars de Ordine Martyrum had already been established in Guildford, as a building built in about 1260 was excavated on the east bank of the river in the 1970s. Eleanor may have incorporated these earlier friars into her new establishment. The actual date of the founding of the new friary is not known. Although Prince Henry was buried in Westminster Abbey, his heart was buried in the Guildford's friary church. On each anniversary of his death it was 'solemnly exposed', so that masses for the repose of his soul could be said.

The original friary building was enlarged and improved with the help of various wealthy benefactors, including the king himself. As well as money, he contributed four oak trees 'fit for timber' and two 'leafless trees' that could be used for fuel. In 1275, the year after his son died, Edward I granted the Dominicans access to the king's park on the other side of the river. Here they planted walnut trees, and the name Walnut Tree Close is a reminder of that time. In return for royal patronage, the friars used their horticultural skills by 'seeking out, trimming and fashioning grounds and gardens about the King's place'.

All friaries followed a similar pattern, with the buildings built around a central courtyard. Behind these buildings and alongside the river were gardens and pastures. The dining room was above the kitchen on the north side, the dormitory above the parlour on the east side and there were a chapter house and sacristy where vestments and equipment were kept. The church was on the south side nearest the town, and the churchyard was the burial place not only of the friars but also of wealthy lay-people. During the 1970s' excavations a lay-person's grave was discovered in the nave. On a lead coffin was inscribed the name Margaret d'Aubeny, and inside were the bones of a woman aged about 20 and possibly those of a baby. This name is not a local one, so her presence here is a mystery.[15]

When Eleanor of Castile died, Edward married Margaret of France, who bore him two sons. On 17 May 1306 Prince Henry's two half-brothers, Thomas and Edmund, were present in Guildford at a mass for his soul. While the friars continued to receive royal funding, many pious noblemen were happy to follow their sovereign's example and give alms to the friars, enabling them to pursue their vocation of preaching and teaching. In 1298 Edward gave the friary six more 'leafless trees' from the royal park, and also gave the friars money for food on several occasions.

On Edward's death in 1307 his son became Edward II. He was very different from his charismatic father, and has been described as Edward I's greatest failure. A weak king, he was eventually deposed after 20 years of poor rule. However, he left one memorial in Guildford. In 1308 Edward granted a charter that gave the right for St Catherine's village, on the south side of the town, to hold a fair every year on 4 October. St Catherine's lay in the parish of St Nicolas's Church and at this time the rector was Richard de Vavncey. He was very forward-looking, and it was he who persuaded the king that the village should have a fair. The charter included an unusual clause. On payment of a small sum to the lord of the manor, all inns were permitted to sell beer without a licence on the Sunday preceding the fair. This day came to be known as Tap-up Sunday, and was greatly appreciated by the villagers, who made good use of the brief relaxation of the licensing laws. Unfortunately this dispensation sometimes attracted outsiders who were not as law-abiding as the villagers. Originally the fair was for selling livestock and household goods, but gradually entertainment was introduced – and eventually predominated.

Richard de Vavncey continued to hold the parishioners' best interests in mind. As he felt that St Nicolas's Church was too far for them to walk every Sunday, he built a chapel-of-ease on the top of St Catherine's Hill in 1317. It is near to what is known as the Pilgrims' Way, an ancient route passing over the North Downs. Despite the name and tradition to the contrary, there seems no evidence that pilgrims used it on their way to Canterbury. The path crossed the River Wey at Ferry Lane, where there was a ferry

17 & 18   *St Catherine's Chapel.*

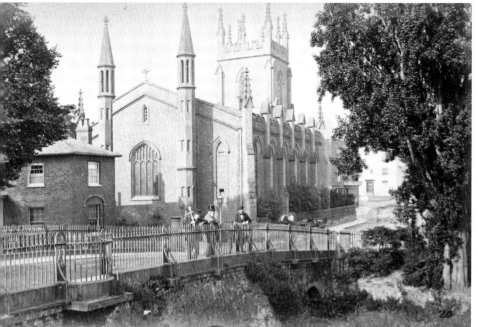

19 *St Nicolas's Church.*

20 *Interior of
St Nicolas Church.*

21 *The ferry at St Catherine's, early 20th century.*

from the Middle Ages. This was only discontinued in the 1960s, and in 1985 a modern footbridge was built across the river.

Trying to continue his parents' connection with the Dominican friary, in 1318 Edward II tried unsuccessfully to carry out his mother's wishes to found a monastery of Dominican sisters, re-inventing the friary for women instead of men. In pursuit of his aim, he wrote 'diverse letters to Rome' and even sent two of the friars, Richard de Burton and Andrew de Aslakeby, to Rome to plead with the pope. One wonders how they felt – as if they had been successful they would have had to leave their friary. But the pope proved adamant and refused to give permission, so the friars continued as before.[16] Edward II did nothing to improve the facilities in the castle, and the friary was used as a royal residence when the king visited Guildford.

Edward became increasingly unpopular, and in 1327 he was forced to abdicate in favour of his 15-year-old son, another Edward, who reigned for 50 years. In 1341 Edward III granted Guildford the right to hold an annual fair in May. This was particularly important for livestock – primarily sheep and horses. So the Guildford area now had two fairs to look forward to – one in May and one in October.

Edward's long reign was dominated by the war with France, known now as the Hundred Years' War, so he had little time to visit Guildford. In 1348 the plague descended on the country, destroying half the population, although Guildford does not appear to have been badly affected. Edward's long reign came to an end in 1367. His son, Edward, the Black Prince, had died in battle, so he was succeeded by his grandson, Richard II, another weak king, who ruled for 22 years. He showed little interest in Guildford and rarely visited. The castle continued to deteriorate and by 1379 it was virtually a ruin. In 1399 the throne was wrested from Richard by his ruthless cousin Henry Bolingbroke, who became Henry IV. His reign was turbulent but he occasionally visited Guildford, staying together with his retinue at the friary. They were not always popular guests: in February 1403 his followers left a gift of 40s. 'to cover the damage done to the house, vessels and gardens'. As the king visited Guildford less and less, his financial support of the friary declined and the monks found it increasingly difficult to support themselves. However, they continued to struggle on until the middle of the following century.

THREE

The Tudors and Stuarts

In 1485 Henry VII granted Guildford its own coat of arms. As the town had been a royal manor for centuries, a twin-towered castle dominated the design. The Tudor roses on either side of the gateway, the key within it and the lion couchant in front also symbolised the royal connection. The following is the heraldic description:

> Sable, on a mount vert a castle with two towers embattled, on each tower a spire surmounted with a ball from the battlements, between the towers a tower triple-towered all argent and charged with an escutcheon quarterly of France and England, under the battlements of the castle two roses in fesse, on the port proper, charged on the centre with a key and portcullised both gold, on the mount before the port a lion couchant gardant of the fourth, on each side the castle in fesse a wool back of the third paleways, the base of the file water proper.[1]

Because wool was produced in such a large quantity in the town, the guild merchant requested that the woolsack be incorporated onto the coat of arms, but this was not granted until the following century.[2]

In 1488, three years after the coat of arms was granted, the king granted the town a charter of incorporation, because

> the said towne is soe decayed and impoverished by the payeing of the fee farm, and by other charges hanging daylie upon the said towne ... we of our special love have graunted to the now mayor and good men of the towne aforesaid and to their successors for ever that the same towne be corporated from henceforth for ever.[3]

22   *Guildford coat of arms.*

His use of the word mayor was the first time the title had been formally used, although the term had been recognised since the late 14th century. The role of the first citizen had changed as the mayor was no longer a member of the royal household but a merchant freely elected by the guild merchant, of which he was then the head. As such, his most important concern was the prosperity of the town.

It was during the reign of Henry's son, Henry VIII, that the mayor and corporation were instructed to wear gowns on formal occasions. Apparently some of them resisted so a fine was imposed. A record in the 'Town Books' of 1536 states that it was 'ordered that the Bailiffe of the towne do accompany the Maior on solemn and public occasions and to wear his gowne to be fined eightpence in default'.[4]

Markets had played an important part in English life for centuries, and Guildford was no exception. Three markets were held each week – the corn market, the cattle market and a general market selling food, household goods and a variety of other wares. The most profitable was the corn market, including wheat for the making of flour, barley for brewing beer and oats to feed animals. A market toll was charged. Porters, who carried the sacks, scooped out a 'pint' of grain, and the money for this swelled the coffers of the corporation. The scoops used were small bowls with handles: two of them, made of copper, were probably Elizabethan, but three bronze ones with iron handles were from an earlier period. They continued to be used until the abolition of the toll.[5]

In 1561 a large market house was built 'beneath the Gild Hall', but eventually it became unsuitable to store the 'grayne accusstimablie sold there',[6] and in 1626 the market was relocated to the *Tunne Inn* on the opposite side of the road, where a wooden canopy was erected to protect the corn. At the rear of the building there was a court room where the annual assizes were held.

The cattle market dominated the High Street. Farmers from the surrounding areas drove their cows, oxen, pigs and sheep into the already bustling town; fishwives sold their fish under the protection of the fish cross, which stood opposite the *Angel Inn*; poultry sellers were squashed into an area between the two inns – the *Tun* and the *White Hart;* vendors in the general market selling a variety of goods found space wherever they could. The arrangement was haphazard and far too crowded for comfort. The fish cross, which had been erected in the Middle Ages, was an obstacle to the free flow of traffic. In 1592 it was decided to remove it 'forthwith' and find 'a convenient place' to build another shelter for the fish market. The cross was indeed removed, but no other edifice was ever erected – 'and the fishwives were forced to make use of the wheat market house'. However, to ease congestion a street off the High Street was commandeered to accommodate some of the market stalls. Known as the Shambles, it lived up to its name as vendors selling shoes, crockery, leather goods and a variety of other wares vied with each other for space in the narrow lane, which still bears the same name.

While the market flourished – albeit in cramped conditions – the friary was struggling to maintain its position. Henry VIII did not visit Guildford as often as some of his predecessors had done. Nevertheless, he 'professed great love and affection for the Friary' and built himself a hunting lodge within its precincts.[7] Then in July 1530 the friary was given a 'reward' of £5, which was renewed in July 1533. It is likely that this was for work done by the friars in the royal gardens and grounds, as they were skilled in horticulture. A large unspecified sum was also paid to a friar named Anserois, no doubt for some service he had rendered the king.

It was at 'the house of the Blackfries' on 2 August 1534 that Henry was present to ratify a treaty with Scotland after the country's abortive attempt to conquer England. Also present were the Scottish ambassador, the Duke of Norfolk; the Bishop of Winchester, in whose diocese Guildford lay; and Thomas Cromwell, Henry's chancellor. But the friary continued to decline and the

23 *Friary, c.1705, from a watercolour said to have been done for the Colwall family.*

24 *Watercolour of the friary in 1816 when used as a cavalry barracks.*

25   *Plan of Friary site.*

26a & b   *Skeletons found on Friary site.*

friars found it increasingly difficult to get enough money even to feed them-selves. On 10 August 1536 John Hilsey, Bishop of Rochester, concerned about their plight, wrote to the king begging him to 'grant the Friars a perpetual alms for the relief of their poverty'.[8] The friars also sent a petition informing the king that their house and the 'place of honour that the King had built within their precincts were now decaying'. Their alms, they told him, had 'of late much fallen off so that they often wanted even food' and, no doubt because of their weakness owing to the lack of food, they were 'unable to serve the king in setting out and trimming and fashioning ground and gardens about the king's place'. They eventually received an 'annuity of 20 marks in pure alms' but the friary and other monasteries were doomed.

In 1537 Henry VIII ordered the dissolution of all monasteries. By this time there were only seven brothers left in the friary, and because of 'the great claim of debts' Henry's hirelings were forced to sell some of the friary's possessions to pay off its creditors. On 10 October 1538 Prior Cobden and 'the Black Friars of Guildford ... without any manner of coercion' surrendered what remained of the friary and its lands to the lord visitor who represented the king. He made an inventory of the possession of 'The Black Freers of Gulforde':

> This Indenture makith mencyon of all the staple remaynning in the house of the Blacke Freerys of Gilforde receevyed by the lord visitor under the lorde privy seale and delyvored to John Daborne mayor and to Daniel Mugge to see and order to the Kingis use with the howse and all appertenances till the kingis plesure be further knownen.[9]

A keeper of the royal park was appointed, and the remains of the friary were converted into a suitable dwelling for the king to use on his occasional visits to the town.

Ironically Henry planned to visit Guildford in 1537, but Thomas Cromwell, Henry's chancellor, received a letter from Sir William, the treasurer of the friary, suggesting that he and his royal master should lodge at the parsonage of St Nicolas 'as the Freres is but a little house and will be sore pestered at the King's being there'. They took his advice. Finally in 1606 the friary building was demolished. In 1630 the entire park was bought for £5,000 by Lord Annandale, the king's keeper. On the site of the friary he built himself a large mansion, but this too was later demolished, and the site had a number of owners over the years. In 1794 it was transformed into a barracks, and new buildings were erected to house 800 men. By 1818 all the buildings had been destroyed, and the site was taken over by various organisations, including a brewery, before its final metamorphosis into a shopping complex in the

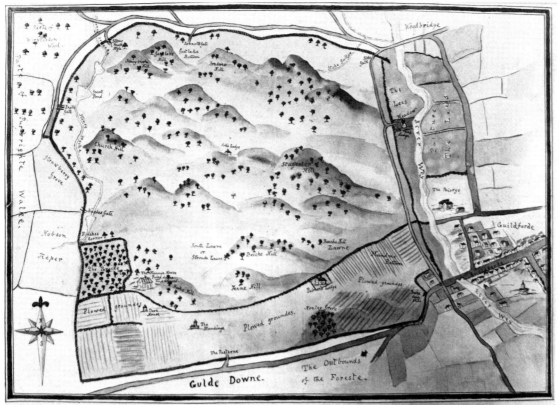

27   *Map of Guildford Park, 1607.*

28   *Bowling Green.*

20th century. During excavations in the 1970s a number of bones from more than 35 bodies were found.

The castle, meanwhile, had fallen into disrepair and was now a prison. In 1612, however, it was given a new lease of life when it was sold to a certain Francis Carter for the princely sum of 26s. Intending to make the keep habitable and live in it, he inserted some Tudor windows but went no further. Instead he built a house beside the western wall of the castle – now Guildford Museum. He also created a bowling green, possibly for the use of his family: bowling had become a fashionable pastime in the 17th century. The bowling green is still kept in pristine condition and is used by the public over 300 years later.

Other buildings that flourished were the inns. Guildford might no longer have a royal residence but it was still an important resting place for travellers, as it was on the main route to London from Southampton, Portsmouth and Winchester. In *The Natural History and Antiquities of the County of Surrey*, published in 1718, John Aubrey wrote that Guildford 'has always been famous for its good Inns and excellent Accommodation for Passengers – the best perhaps in England'.

29   *The* Angel Inn.

The Angel Posting House and Livery Stables, in the centre of the High Street, was built during the Middle Ages. A recently excavated stone-vaulted undercroft with an original spiral staircase dates from about 1300 (see p.13). The first recorded owner was Pancras Chamberlyn. In a document dated 21 June 1527 he sold the building to Sir Christopher More for £10. Sir Christopher died in 1545 and his son, William, inherited the *Angel*. On 20 June 1551 he conveyed the building to Margaret Danyel as a marriage settlement. Later the lease was sold to John Hole, a shoemaker, who then passed it on to John Astret, a yeoman from Cranleigh. When he died on 8 June 1606 he bequeathed it to his son Thomas. Documentary evidence at this time refers for the first time to the *Angel* as an 'Inn'. In the early part of the 17th century it was partly rebuilt, which gave the opportunity to introduce distinctive Jacobean woodwork and panelling. In 1685 a brick fireplace and a minstrel gallery were added. In 1688 the government presented a large octagonal 'parliamentary clock'. Still in good working order, it hangs on the wall beside the main staircase.

30   *The parliamentary clock at the* Angel.

The *Angel* became an increasingly popular staging post for travellers, and the 13th-century undercroft was used to stable their horses. Many famous people are rumoured to have stayed there, although there is not always more than circumstantial evidence. Sir Francis Drake would undoubtedly have made use of the *Angel*'s facilities on his frequent journeys between Portsmouth and London. Tradition suggests that Samuel Pepys also visited on several occasions. More recent visitors probably included Dr Samuel Johnson, James Boswell, Lord Nelson, Jane Austen, William Pitt and Charles Dickens.

Another visitor who definitely left his mark on the *Angel* was Oliver Cromwell. During the Civil War he billeted soldiers there; the undercroft was transformed into a hospital. The soldiers were expensive to feed, and with little monetary help from Cromwell the *Angel* was soon bankrupt. Fortunately it recovered after the Restoration of Charles II, when wealthier guests again used the inn to break their journey; once more their horses were stabled in the undercroft.

There were a number of other inns plying their lucrative trade during the 17th century: the *White Hart*, the *Bear*, the *George*, the *Red Lion*, the *Tun*, the *White Lion*, the *Star*, the *King's Head* and the *Crown*. It was usual for keepers of alehouses and inns to brew ale themselves and sell it to their customers.[10] Because wool was the staple industry of the town, 'every alehouse-keeper was obliged, by an ordinance of the Corporation to have a sign board with a *wool-sack* painted thereon, hung up at his door, under the penalty of 6s. 8d. in case of neglect'.[11] The inns were all very popular – particularly on Twelfth Night, 6 January, when the Pilgrim Morris Men performed a mummers' play. They moved from inn to inn, starting at the end of the High Street and working their way to the top. The first port of call was the *Star* at the corner of Quarry Street. Built in about 1600, it was a timber-framed building with a projecting upper floor, or jetty. Here the wassail bowl was filled with 'seasonally spiced liquor'. A fruit cake was cut and shared among the mummers. One slice contained a bean, and the recipient of this was elected as the king of misrule.

Three crosses were marked on one of the timbers at the *Star*. Their meaning has been lost but there are three possibilities: the three ages of man, the Trinity, or past, present and future. Whatever their origin, they were supposed to bring good luck to all who passed beneath them. The 'king' ordered the mummers to perform the play underneath them, and they were then renewed for another year. On one occasion the mummers omitted to include the *King's Head* on their rounds and the inn suffered some subsidence! The mummers would proceed from inn to inn charging their tankards in each one, so by the time they reached the top of the High Street they must have been very drunk.

The Quakers became established in Guildford in about 1650, the year after Charles I was executed and Oliver Cromwell started his rise to fame. However, when Charles II was restored to the throne in 1660, persecution of the Quakers began and they struggled to survive. As they usually met in private houses, it was not difficult to keep a low profile, but nevertheless many were imprisoned during this period.

However, in 1672 the strict laws were relaxed and the following year the Quakers were given a parcel of land near the top of the High Street, on which they built a meeting house. This area is now known as Quaker's Acre. The meeting house continued to be used until 1805 when a new one was built, and the garden was used as a cemetery. A speaker's tree in the centre was used for public speaking. The area was finally presented to the town in 1927 and now, with its two wooden seats and tranquil atmosphere, it provides a small oasis of peace in the midst of a busy town.

There are no records of the building of the medieval Guildhall, but there are references to it during the reign of Edward III in the 14th century. A donation of 13s. 6d. was made for repairs to the 'Gildeford Gild Hall'. There are also several references during the reign of Henry VIII. In 1525 some repair work was done, but there is no record of what it was – although the wages and materials were detailed by the workmen. 'They be the costes done by me Wylym Hamond to the Yeld Hall'.

31 *Guildford High Street with clock and Guildhall.*

In 1683 there appear to have been some major changes to the Guildhall, and £229 was donated by a number of prominent Guildford citizens. The council chamber was erected over the entrance and partly over the Guildhall. A manor house at Stoughton had recently been demolished, and the very fine 14th-century mantelpiece which had been in the hall was relocated to the new council chamber. It was important that it was preserved, as it was a fine example of medieval work in sculptured stone. It was relevant to its time, as the artist carved illustrations representing the four 'humours' that were believed to make up the human body: Sanguine, Choleric, Phlegmatic and Melancholic. The first, entitled 'Sanguinus', shows a lover and his mistress; a warrior with his weapons represents 'Cholericus'; a fisherman sitting in his boat is 'Phlegmaticus'; and the final figure who sits alone gazing into space is 'Melancolicus'. At the end of the 17th century David Irish, a physician who lived in Stoke, published *Animadversa Astrologica*, in which he suggested that the four 'humours' were influenced by the four seasons.[12]

Tradition says that the famous clock with pride of place outside the Guildhall was given to the town by one John Aylward – but the details of the donation are vague and not documented. It is said that, as a 'foreigner' who had not been born in Guildford, Aylward was refused permission to trade in the town; therefore he set up his business as a clockmaker outside the borough, in what is now Mount Street. Determined to obtain the freedom to have his workshop within the borough, he made a handsome clock which he presented to the guild merchant. When they received this, Aylward was apparently able to become a member of the guild, and settle in the High Street opposite the Guildhall. Although the date on the casing of the clock is 1683, the clock itself was probably made much earlier, when Aylward was working as a clockmaker.[13] It was written in 1561 that 'the mercate house was builded, with the clock and dyall', so this may be the date at which the clock was presented. It was obviously much appreciated, as a sum of money was set aside for the 'maytenance and continuance of the said clock'.

The Guildhall was responsible for the storing and maintenance of some of the town's treasures. Only a few towns in England had the privilege of being the custodian of the standard weights and measures, and Guildford was one of them. In 1514 'there were presented before the Mayor all manner of weyttes and mesuris belonging to the Hall'. This was presumably so they could be checked to see that all were present and correct. Unfortunately 'the pownd weygtt [was] lakkying at the sayd day'.[14] When these standard measures were called in at the beginning of the 16th century, Queen Elizabeth presented the town with four bronze copies engraved with her initials. These, dated 1602, were the bushel, the gallon, the quart and the pint.

Armour and arms were also stored in the Guildhall. The wealthy men of the town were responsible for providing the arms, and in times of unrest the monarch was able to call upon the town to provide both men and ammunition to quell any disturbances. In 1547 three men 'appoynted to serve the Kynge for this towne of Guldeford' were given permission to use some of the armour: 'Thes iii harnesses with wepons accordingl ar taken owt of the xvi payre of harnes in ye Yelde Hall so yt at this daye remayneth but xiii payre.'[15] The arms and armour were checked regularly and a stipend was paid every year 'for mending and scowring the common armour'.

Another weapon housed in the Guildhall but used solely for ceremonial purposes was the sword of state. Traditionally this was presented to the town by the sovereign, and it was carried in front of the mayor on all important occasions. Guildford is one of the few towns to be accorded the privilege of owning a state sword. It is not known when this honour was conferred but it was probably at the end of the 16th century, when Elizabeth was on the throne. Another royal privilege was the right for the mayor and aldermen to wear robes of scarlet, the royal colour, which was granted by charter in 1586 by Queen Elizabeth: 'That it shall and may be lawful for the Maior and Aldermen of the said towne on all holidays, convocations, public meetings and solemnities, for their greater ornament and honour, to wear gownes made of scarlet cloth'.[16]

In 1587 Elizabeth reluctantly signed the death warrant of her cousin, Mary Queen of Scots: while Mary lived there would always be Catholics plotting to remove the Protestant Elizabeth from the throne and replace her with her Catholic cousin. Mary was executed the same year at Fotheringay Castle. However, when Elizabeth died in 1604 she was succeeded by Mary's son, James VI of Scotland, who now also became James I of England. He had been separated from his mother and brought up as a Protestant, so he was acceptable to the English nobles. However, Catholic resentment had not gone away, and there were still a number of Catholics in England who were determined to see a Catholic on the throne.

It was not long before a group of 12 young Catholic men hatched a plot to blow up the Houses of Parliament when the new king opened it. In May 1604 they rented a house next door to the House of Lords and started tunnelling underneath, but to their annoyance the opening of Parliament was postponed until February of the following year, then again until November 1605. They were still determined to carry out their plans, but they abandoned the tunnel when they realised that there was an empty cellar directly under the House of Lords, an ideal place in which to store 36 barrels of gunpowder, which were surreptitiously ferried across the Thames.

The conspirators were delighted with their plan but one of them, Francis Tresham, was concerned about the safety of his brother-in-law, Lord Monteagle, who sat in Parliament. Trying not to give away the plot, he wrote a letter warning him of 'a terrible blow' that was about to fall. The others were horrified and hurriedly left London, leaving Guy Fawkes to mount guard over the gunpowder and detonate it on 5 November once he was sure the king and Parliament had taken their seats.

Lord Monteagle, suspicious of the 'terrible blow', did not keep the letter to himself. The warning was taken seriously, the cellar was searched, the gunpowder discovered and Guy Fawkes arrested. He snarled that 'one of his objects had been to blow the Scots back again into Scotland'. Although it was the middle of the night, the king was aroused and told of the plot. Guy Fawkes was tortured and all the conspirators were rounded up, but four of them were killed when they resisted arrest. The other eight were tried the following January in Westminster Hall. After being hanged, their heads were displayed on pikes as a warning to any others who might venture on a similar course. The king and the whole country rejoiced at the failure of the plot, and James ordered that the discovery of one of 'the greatest treasons that ever were plotted in England' should be remembered with special prayers of thanksgiving in the churches. From that grew the tradition of celebrating 5 November with fireworks and bonfires, on which an effigy of Guy Fawkes was burnt. The resulting celebrations sometimes got out of hand, as they did in Guildford during the 19th century (see Chapter Six).

While transport on the roads was improving, the river was not idle. It was already driving the mills, but sometimes it overflowed its banks. The low-lying lands at Sutton Place were frequently flooded, to the frustration of the owner, Sir Richard Weston. An intelligent aristocrat who had ideas far ahead of his time, he was determined to do something about it. Always interested in the potential of canals, it was he who erected the first lock at Stoke.

Sir Richard also felt that the whole navigation of the River Wey could be improved, so that river barges could sail from Guildford right through to the River Thames. In 1635 he submitted his elaborate plans to the king, Charles I, who graciously granted him a commission to fulfil his dream. Unfortunately the Civil War, which erupted in 1642, interrupted the commencement of the scheme: Sir Richard was a Roman Catholic and his sympathies lay with the royalist cause. Meanwhile the corn and timber trades continued to thrive. In 1648-9 new timber mill buildings were built near the river, incorporating four pairs of stones and a fulling mill.

During this time Sir Richard Onslow of West Clandon, a staunch Puritan, set up a parliamentary committee in Guildford.[17] He was swift to stamp out any royalist leanings among the citizens, but fortunately the town escaped any actual fighting. However, it suffered from the increased taxation levied to support the army and also from the cost of billeting soldiers in the area, who remained even after the end of the Civil War. The citizens of Guildford resented this, and in May 1648 a public meeting was held in the *White Hart* to air their grievances. This resulted in Parliament being urged to make peace with the king. However, in spite of this apparent support for the return of the monarchy, Guildford showed little interest in a royalist uprising elsewhere in Surrey the following year. It was unsuccessful, and Parliament retained its power.

Meanwhile, Sir Richard Weston had not given up his Wey navigation plans. In 1651 his powers of persuasion bore fruit when an Act of Parliament was passed that enabled the building of the navigation to go ahead. 'The Mayor and Approved Men of Guildford' were the authority appointed to oversee the scheme. Its acceptance may have been aided by the fact that Sir Richard diplomatically engaged a partner, James Pitson, who was a major in Cromwell's army. They did not waste time, and by 1653 the Wey Navigation was completed. Nine miles of canals were dug and 12 locks, including a 'pound' lock, were constructed. The total length of the Navigation was 15½ miles, and the town prospered greatly as a result of it. Barges carrying cargoes of grain, timber, coal, corn, flour and even gunpowder were able to travel between London's docks and Guildford. The corn trade continued to thrive as the Wey Navigation provided easy transport to London, but the wool trade declined rapidly.

Sadly Sir Richard Weston died before the work was completed and it was his son, George, who consequently became responsible for it. Things did not go smoothly for him. Almost immediately after its completion the scheme ran into financial difficulties. The final cost was double the original estimate and the administration of funds had not been as efficient as it should have been. This resulted in a great deal of bad feeling between the partners and others who were involved. Accusations and counter-accusations abounded, and James Pitson was accused of embezzlement. It was George Weston, however, who was the ultimate sufferer. Forced to sell his shares in the business, he was then imprisoned for his father's debts. The unsavoury dispute continued for several years and it was not until 1671 that order was restored by the passing of an Act that appointed two judges and a body of trustees to oversee the Navigation. Under the new governing body it prospered.

The ambitious project had not always met with unreserved support in the town. In fact it may have been so unpopular 'that, as tradition informs us, the work of the day was destroyed in the night by the labouring classes till at length it became necessary to have night guards'.[18] There is no concrete evidence that this was the case, but taking note of the reaction of some of its citizens, the corporation applied for and received permission to charge a toll of a penny for every ton of merchandise carried upstream. As the navigation prospered, the method of transporting the barges improved. Originally they had been rowed; then, as the size of the cargoes and consequently the barges increased, they were hauled along by men on the towpath. This ultimately gave way to horse-drawn barges, which were still in use in the early 20th century.

When Charles II was restored to the throne in 1660 little changed in Guildford, and its citizens continued to live in peace with their neighbours. The king did not interfere in the running of the town. However, an important development after the Restoration that affected Guildford was the development of Portsmouth as a naval base. It took two days to travel from Portsmouth to London, and travellers stayed at Guildford *en route*. The inns did a flourishing trade, and Guildford became a busy place.

In 1673 the mayor was offered a solid gold chain of office by Arthur Onslow of West Clandon, who was the High Steward of Guildford. A three-inch oval medallion was suspended from the chain. On one side was engraved the royal arms of Charles II flanked on either side with the king's initials. The other side, dated MDCLXXII, was bordered by laurel leaves and carried a shield bearing the Onslow arms. This was surrounded by the words: *Semper Fidelis Festina Lente* and *Ex dono Arthuri Onslow Armigeri*. An entry in the town's records refers to the gift:

> Memorand. That on the third day of March in the six & twentyeth year of the reigne of our most gracious Soverayne King Charles the second Kind of England etc. 1673 Arthur Onslow of West Clandon in the County of Surrey Esquire High Steward of this towne did then give to the Mayor and approved men of the sayd Towne and their successors a faire chayne of gold, Double linked with a medal of massey Gold; whereon his Majesties Armes are curiously engraven and on the reverse the Armes of the said Mr. Onslow. In token of our gratittude and memory whereof we have caused this entry amoung our Records. Optima beneficiorium custus est ipsa memoria beneficiorum.[19]

However, the chain does not appear to have been received by the mayor until the following year, when an entry read: 'Given Mr. Onslow's servants when the gold Chayne was sent, £3.15.6.'

Other important things had been happening in Guildford during the reigns of the Tudors and Stuarts. In 1509 a wealthy merchant, Robert Beckingham, 'a London Member of the Grocers' Company', died and in his will bequeathed to Guildford one of its most important educational institutions.[20] As he lived and died in the parish of St Olave, in Southwark, his interest in Guildford is intriguing, as he does not appear to have a specific link with the town. However, he was friends with a certain Thomas Polsted who lived in Stoke parish, which bordered the town, so perhaps Polsted influenced him; or perhaps, as a businessman, Beckingham had traded with Guildford. Whatever the reason, he was obviously attracted to the town and was close to Polsted, who was an executor of Beckingham's will; this was dated 3 November 1509.[21] In his own will Polsted had 'bequathed money for perpetural Masses to be said for not only *his* family but also for Robert Bechingham and his wife Elizabeth'.

Beckingham died on 10 December 1509, the month after making his will in which, among other bequests, he stipulated that a chantry chapel should be built. There, prayers for the souls of himself and his wife would be said in perpetuity. The money for this, which was worth £4 13s. 4d. annually, came from rent from land Beckingham owned; it was left in trust to the Brotherhood of Our Lady in Southwark, the parish where Beckingham spent his life. However, there were conditions imposed. The will stated that if the building of the chapel had not started within two years of his death the money was to be used 'to make a free schole at the Town of Guldford'. This condition was not met, so the executors proceeded to comply with Beckingham's instructions. The land he had owned was transferred to the governing body, the Mayor and Approved Men, and on 4 May 1512 the 'free school' was established with six pupils and one teacher.[22] The trust deed stated that 'there should be a sufficient school master there always from henceforth to keep the said school and freely to teach all children being in the same school'.[23] There were no instructions in the trust deed as to what should be taught. However, it was stipulated that 'the children should say psalms each morning and evening, as well as evening prayers for the souls of Robert and Elizabeth Beckingham and all other benefactors of the school'.[24] The deed also invested the Mayor and Approved Men of the town with 'the duty of ever afterwards maintaining the school'. They apparently took their duties very seriously, as on 3 September 1520 they gave to the school a parcel of land adjoining the castle ditch. A schoolhouse and a master's house were built on it.[25] Beckingham's will had stipulated that the school should be endowed as a chantry, so that daily prayers could be said in its chapel for the souls of himself and his wife. The school had a master, who was paid an annual salary of £6, and there were not more than 30 pupils. It continued to provide a basic education for its pupils until 1547, when Edward VI confiscated chantry properties.

Concerned about losing their free school, the town councillors petitioned the king for a charter and an income so that it did not have to close. To their delight Edward granted a royal charter and an annual sum of £20. On 27 January 1553 the 'Schola Regia Grammaticalis Edvardi Sexi' was formally established 'for the Education, Institution and Instruction of Boys and Youths in Grammar at all future times'. The charter invested the Mayor and Approved Men together with the warden of the king's manor with the authority to appoint masters to the school. Three years earlier Henry Polsted, Thomas's son, had presented the school with a gift of 'two messuages, near the pillory in the parish of St Mary for its maintenance worth £4 15s. a year'.

When Protestant Edward VI died in 1553, his sister Mary was determined to bring back the Catholic faith. In 1555 she instructed that all schoolmasters were to be licensed by bishops – a power retained by further monarchs.[26] However, if the school were to develop more buildings were needed, and on 28 July 1555 a large piece of open land was bought; an additional three acres were bought on 3 September the same year, but it was not until 1557 that the building started. This was to consist of a large schoolroom, a common room, a dormitory for boarders and houses for the master and usher. The schoolroom was eventually completed, but there was not enough accommodation for the master and usher, and funds ran low as the work became increasingly expensive.

In 1569 John Austen and William Hamonde, two of Guildford's wealthy citizens, decided to raise capital to build two new wings and a connecting gallery. Work started in 1571, but progress was slow and had not been completed before John Austen died. His son, George, who became Mayor of Guildford, 'knowing what travell and paynes the said John Austen my father had taken to buyld the same, and seeinge howe likely it was to fall to utter decay, I did consider what course might be taken to bring the same to perfection'.[27] He wasted no time in persuading the local gentry to part with their money for such a good cause – that of educating the young. He was obviously very persuasive, and in 1586 the building work was finally completed and the Royal Grammar School had a building that befitted its academic aspirations. In 1574 it had been given a priceless gift when an old boy of the school, John Parkhurst, who had become Bishop of Norwich, donated his valuable collection of theological books to the school. A gallery was renovated and converted into a library; the books were chained to the bookshelves so that no light-fingered pupils were tempted to remove them. Today this chained library is housed in the headmaster's study.

Originally the school contained not more than 100 boys. At first places in the school were free, although the boys paid 2d. a quarter for brooms and candles. Eventually there were fewer free places and parents had to pay for their sons' education. The pupils were given a thorough grounding in Latin and Greek and, with the advent of Protestant Elizabeth, the doctrine of the Protestant religion was instilled in them.

In 1596 George Austen decided that records of the building of the school should be kept and he started his *Monument*. This was a detailed and lucidly written account of every incident related to the building of the school. It throws great light on Guildford society in the 16th century and gives an insight into the characters of the men who were instrumental in making sure that the Grammar School survived.

The Royal Grammar School has another claim to fame, as it has been suggested that the first mention of cricket was connected with the school. In 1598 there was a dispute over some land adjoining it, and

> John Derrick, Gent, one of the Queen's Majesties Coroners of the County of Surrey aged fifty-nine saith this land before mentioned ... lay waste and ... when he was a scholar of the Free School of Guildford he and several of his fellows did run and play there at *Crickett* and other plaies.[28]

In 1608 George Austen prepared some statutes for the running of the school. These were approved by the Bishop of Winchester, in whose diocese Guildford lay. They included the clause: 'No child within the town who is worthy of admission should be refused admission.' Over the next two centuries the school had its problems but survived; by the end of the 19th century it had established itself as an excellent school with high standards. It remained a boys' school and in the 20th century the number of pupils increased, while there was great academic improvement. As the education system in the county changed, the Royal Grammar School also had to change. In September 1977 it became an independent boys' school and since then has continued to thrive. Today it caters for around 900 boys and provides an excellent all-round education fitting its pupils to play their part in the 21st century.

In 1579 another educational establishment had come into being. One Thomas Baker was granted some land at the top of the High Street on which he planned to build a market house at a cost to himself of £300. He would receive the receipts from this during his lifetime, but after his death the money was used to found a school for children of poor parents. There would be one master, who would receive £100 a year. D.M. Stanley, who wrote a history of the Royal Grammar School, suggested that students from Baker's school might then go on to the Grammar School: 'It had always been necessary for boys to read and write before being admitted to the Grammar School.' At first the school had no permanent home. To begin with, it functioned in an attic room of the market house but then moved around – even using a room in the tower of Holy Trinity Church.

One of Guildford's most famous sons was George Abbot, who was educated at the Grammar School. His family had originally come from Suffolk, and there are records of Abbots in Chelsworth in 1260. It was not, however, until the 16th century that they took up residence in Guildford.

32 *Royal Grammar School.*

33 *Royal Grammar School – rear view.*

George's grandfather, Thomas Abbot, a clothworker, moved from Chelsworth to Hawkesdon and it was his son, Maurice, also a clothier, who eventually moved to Guildford. He married Alice Marsh at St Mary's Church, Guildford, on 30 June 1548, and they produced five sons. The family lived in a cottage near the bridge over the River Wey not far from St Nicolas's Church. George, their fourth son, was born in 1562. All of the boys had distinguished careers but their origins were undoubtedly humble. On a wall in Holy Trinity Church there is a brass plaque commemorating the family.

There is a fascinating legend about George's birth. While his mother was pregnant with him she had a dream. In it she was told that if she ate a pike during her pregnancy the child would become famous. She forgot about the dream, but a few days later when she drew out a bucket of water from the river she was amazed to see a pike floating in it. Remembering what she had been told, she concluded that she had been sent a sign. She cooked the fish and ate it, and there is no doubt that the son who was born shortly afterwards became the most famous of all her ambitious sons. He was baptised soon after his birth in St Nicolas's Church. While the future archbishop was still a toddler, the family moved to the other side of the river and took up residence in Holy Trinity parish.

The story of George's birth became widely known and attracted the attention of three wealthy godparents, who, realising that the boy had potential and being influenced by the legend, decided to sponsor his education. He was given a free place at the Royal Grammar School. Two curates from the church were masters at the school and they may have influenced their pupil. While there, the young George showed a particular aptitude for ancient languages – Latin, Greek, Hebrew and even Aramaic, the language Christ himself spoke. At the time these were not considered 'dead' languages because they were vital to the understanding of the Bible: the Old Testament had originally been written in Hebrew and the New Testament in Greek. In the fourth century A.D. Jerome had translated the Bible from its original tongues into Latin. Known as the Vulgate, the work had taken him several years. George's understanding of ancient languages was to prove invaluable later in his life when he was involved, with others, in translating the Scriptures.

Having distinguished himself at school, Abbot entered Balliol College, Oxford, in 1579 and continued to make his mark. On 31 May 1582 he was awarded a Bachelor of Arts degree and in November of the following year he was elected a Fellow of Balliol College; on 17 December 1585 he became a Master of Arts. He was admitted as a Bachelor of Theology in 1594 and as a Doctor of Divinity in March 1599; in September the same year he was elected

34   *Portrait of George Abbot.*

35   *George Abbot's tomb in Holy Trinity Church.*

Master of University College. Abbot was determined that his students should not be ignorant of the world around them, and in 1599 he published *A Brief Description of the Whole World*; this was very popular and was reprinted a number of times. The latest edition, produced by Tony Richmond, the current Master of Abbot's Hospital, was published in 2011.

Abbot became vice-chancellor of the university in 1600 and then again in 1603 and 1605. On 6 March 1600 he received his first ecclesiastical appointment, being installed as Dean of Winchester – although there is no evidence that he spent much time there. However, this appointment enabled him to become more closely involved with Church affairs.

In 1603 Abbot met James I for the first time: as vice-chancellor, he was deputed to go to Woodstock to greet the

36   *Statue of George Abbot at the top of the High Street.*

king on behalf of the university. Later Abbot won the favour of the sovereign by advising him on theological issues. James wished to unite the Churches of England and Scotland, but the Presbyterian Scots were not happy to accept the consecration of bishops, which to them suggested a return to the rule of the papacy. Abbot was able to convince them that this was not the case, as the leaders of the English Church also had no wish to submit to the pope. Thirteen bishops were duly consecrated.

Abbot's linguistic gifts were soon put to good use when the king had an idea that he hoped would bring the two churches together. In 1603 he summoned clerics from both sides of the border to a conference at Hampton Court and informed them that he wanted a new translation of the Bible that would be available for everyone. At first this idea found little support, but James's powers of persuasion ultimately triumphed. As Whitgift, the current Archbishop of Canterbury, was ill, it fell to Richard Bancroft, the Bishop of London, to hand pick a team of academics to undertake the mammoth task. George Abbot was one of those chosen.

Eventually, after some disagreement about how the work was to be done, the scholars came to an agreement: earlier translations were to be consulted, there should be no radical changes, the traditional language of the Church should be used and the translation should be scrupulously accurate. George Abbot worked on the Gospels, the Acts of the Apostles and Revelation. The translation took seven years to complete, and both the king and the translators from both sides of the border were pleased with the result. The Authorised Version of the King James Bible was published in 1611. It was used exclusively for almost 300 years, until other translations proliferated in the late 19th and 20th centuries.

In 1609 Abbot received his first bishopric. On 27 May he was consecrated in Lambeth Palace as the Bishop of Coventry and Lichfield; two years later he achieved the highest office in the Church of England, when on 16 May 1611 he was enthroned as Archbishop of Canterbury. In 1613 he fell out of favour with the king, as he refused to compromise his principles by supporting James in his approval of the particularly scandalous divorce of the Earl of Essex.

Despite his high office, Abbot had not forgotten his roots, and he was determined to do something to help the poor of his native town. His original idea was to help to restore the ailing cloth industry in Guildford, and he wrote to the Mayor of Guildford enclosing £100 from which interest-free loans were to be made to poor workmen so that they could restore their looms. In 1618 he started his preparations for a 'hospital', which was to be a gift to the people of the town 'out of my love to the place of my birth'. The word hospital has the same root as hospitality and, as this was a Christian duty, hospitals were founded by the Church to offer care and shelter to those in need; eventually it also became necessary to care for those who were sick. Abbot's Hospital retains its original meaning, as it is not a hospital in the modern sense.

The establishment was to provide living accommodation for single, unemployed men and women of good health and character who were over 60 and had been born in Guildford, or had lived in the city for 20 years. Preference was given to those who had held office in the town or who had served in the armed forces. Abbot also stipulated that anyone connected with his family should be eligible for a place, and he reserved the right to choose the prospective residents himself.

Abbot appointed three trustees: Sir Nicholas Kempe, who was steward of the episcopal manors of Farnham; William Baker of Lambeth, his secretary; and Morris Abbot, his brother. In their name he purchased a site comprising land which ran from the top of the High Street to North Street and associated buildings. One of these was the *Half Moon Inn*, which was purchased from Robert Pune for £350 and later demolished. Property to the east of the inn was owned by Henry Astrete, who sold it to the trustees for £100; this too was demolished.

Local bricks were used for the new building, and in 1618 Abbot instructed George Austen, the MP for Guildford, to buy timber to the value of £100 0s. 6d. On April 1619 the archbishop laid the foundation stone of his new hospital, the design of which was modelled on that of an Oxford or Cambridge college. Abbot required a very high standard, and the oak from Cranleigh and Chiddingfold was intricately carved to his specification. The entrance was through an impressive tower, on the archway of which was inscribed '*Deus nobis haiec otia Fecit*' (God made this for our rest). On the huge oak doors were George Abbot's initials and his coat of arms. The gateway led on to a quadrangle, with rooms for the residents on either side. The west side had single rooms for 12 brothers, as they were called, while the sisters on the other side had only eight rooms, because in the corner was the master's lodging, where Abbot stayed when the foundation was nearing completion. On the right of the central path was the chapel, which played an important part in the hospital's life. The stained-glass windows told the story of Jacob – perhaps a compliment to the reigning King James. In their *History of the County of Surrey* Manning and Bray comment:

> For the better government of this Society, it is also provided by the Statutes that divine service be performed in the Chapel of the Hospital *twice* in every day, by the Master, Vice-Master, or one of the Brethren appointed by the former; and that every member, who is able, do daily attend the same, and do also partake of the Lord's Supper at least *three* times in every year. Defaulters, in proportion to their offence, are to be admonished, mulcted, (fined) or expelled.[29]

37 & 38 *Through the arch at Abbot's Hospital.*

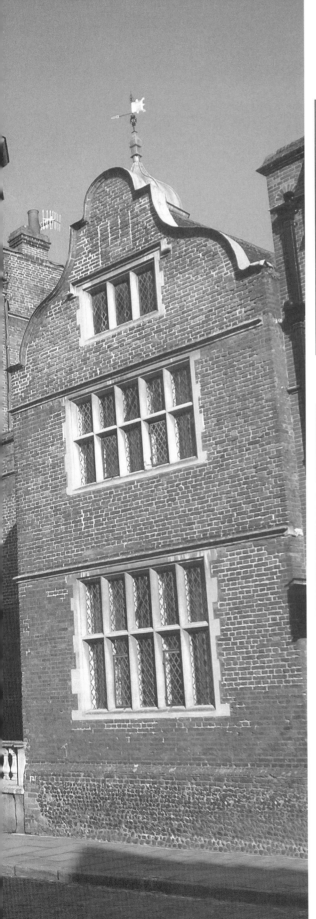

39 & 40   *The Refectory in Abbot's Hospital.*

41   *Abbot's Hospital.*

42   *George Abbot's coat of arms.*

Residents were also expected to attend the nearby Holy Trinity Church on frequent occasions.

At the end of the quadrangle was the common hall where the residents had their meals, which were cooked in a kitchen in the basement. Vegetables, grown in the garden, supplemented any meat that was bought. Out of the 2s. 6d. they were given each week the residents paid 4d. a day for the meal. During the year there were special celebratory meals at Christmas, Easter, Whitsun and on the founder's birthday in October. At the top of a spiral staircase was the strongroom, or 'evidence room', where all important documents were held. Deeds of Abbot's properties, the seal and Abbot's other valuables were kept there. Abbot was a wealthy man, who had bought a number of farms for which he charged rent. In 1628 two huge chests, each with three locks, were made for extra security. To make it even more secure the key of each lock was held by a different person. In one of the chests £100 was always kept for the day-to-day running of the hospital.

By 1621 most of the building work had been completed, and in July of that year Abbot stayed there briefly. By October 1622 the hospital was ready to receive its first residents. That month Abbot celebrated his 60th birthday, and this seemed an appropriate time for the inauguration of the new foundation, which was to be called the Hospital of the Blessed Trinity. James I issued letters patent, and on 29 October a service was held in the chapel to celebrate the hospital's royal charter.

Richard Abbot, one of George's brothers, who had remained in Guildford, was installed as the first master. He was 73 and had been a widower for 12 years, so he was eligible to fill the post. On the same day the first residents were admitted. These six brothers, as they were called, were George Burges, Gregory Frye, Richard Butcher, George Kitchiner, John Rapley and James Seaman. Abbot had hoped that Richard Pardye, who had been a servant in his parents' home, would be able to be one of the brothers, but as he was married this was not possible. The following year on 14 March 1623 the first sisters were admitted. All widows, they were Joan Rapley, Emlin Martin, Winifred Harte and Jane Heath. The residents had to wear blue gowns with a silver badge in the shape of an archbishop's mitre on the left sleeve. A new gown was made for them every two years. The master had 'a large Gowne' but the brothers and sisters were given 'a reasonable gowne according to the tallnesse or stature of the partie that is to weare it'.

To ensure that the hospital would be run on the right lines, Abbot devised a set of rules with penalties for those who broke them. Alcohol was forbidden, no 'swine or other noisome beast' was to be kept in the garden, and 'for the better preserving of all the glasse in the Howse' no dog was permitted within the hospital precincts. All his rules were intended to make life pleasant for the brothers and sisters. He even made provision for two of the sisters to be responsible for the care of the other inmates, and paid them 6s. 8d. a year for this service. To make sure that everything was done according to his wishes he declared himself a 'Visitor' of the hospital and made periodic inspections. Future Archbishops of Canterbury retained the title, and regularly checked the running of the hospital. On 26 June 1624, for the sum of 5s., Abbot passed over the hospital and its lands to the master and brethren.

Abbot had not given up his original idea of a 'manufacture' to resurrect the wool industry in Guildford. He erected a large building behind the hospital, and from his rents he planned to run his new venture. The financial documents were to be kept in the strongroom in the hospital, but Abbot stipulated that they were not to be 'mingled' with the hospital's accounts.

When the first master, Richard Abbot, died on 2 March 1630, Abbot appointed Jasper Yardley in his place. Yardley had worked for Archbishop Bancroft, who preceded Abbot; for the last 10 years he had been warden of a John Whitgift's Hospital in Croydon. Whitgift, Archbishop of Canterbury from 1583 until his death in 1604, had laid the foundation stone of this latter charitable institution on 22 March 1596, and it was this that had inspired Abbot to provide a similar foundation in Guildford.

Money had been given to Richard Abbot for the management of the 'manufacture' but it was left to Jasper Yardley to operate the scheme. He decided that it would be better to make linen rather than wool so that it did not interfere with the town trade. In April 1630, for £20, he rented some land on which flex and hemp could be grown. This was harvested in August, an instructor was appointed and linen was made. Some of the first to be made was used for covering the two long tables in the Common Hall. In July 1632 George Abbot made a will in which he made the Mayor of Guildford and other borough officers responsible for the 'manufacture'. Sadly linen-making did not continue after 1633, as the venture cost more to run that it made and there was little demand for the linen. It was decided to make woollen cloth instead, and in November 1638 the gowns that the brethren wore were made there. Part of the hospital garden was rented for 1s. 8d. a year and used for the racks on which the cloth dried after being dyed. With difficulty the 'manufacture' continued to function until 1655 when it finally foundered; the remaining income from the endowment was used for small grants to poor workmen in the town. The building was kept in good repair, and was eventually used as a union workhouse for the three Guildford parishes.

Abbot's clerical duties kept him away from Guildford, but his fondness for his native town never wavered. He spent time in his palace in Croydon, and he was there when he fell further out of favour with the king. A convinced Puritan, he held strong views about the sacredness of the Sabbath. When in 1618 James issued a decree relaxing some of the strict rules in force, Abbot refused to have it read in the church in Croydon.

Then in 1621 something happened that was to cast a cloud over the rest of Abbot's life. His health had been failing, and he went to Branshill House in Hampshire to recuperate. His friend, Lord Zouche, had recently added a chapel to his house and invited the Archbishop to consecrate it. This he did, and afterwards he stayed on for a short time. Although he had no skill in hunting, he was persuaded to join a hunting party and went out armed with a crossbow. Because his aim was poor he shot a gamekeeper, Peter Hawkins, by accident. The arrow only pierced the man's arm, but lack of any medical aid caused him to bleed to death very quickly.

Abbot's enemies, of whom there were many, accused him of murder and demanded his immediate disqualification from office. Abbot, devastated, retired to Guildford to await his fate. In spite of their disagreements, James accepted that the incident had been an accident, and Abbot returned to court, although he took less part in affairs of state. The incident remained with him and, no doubt, contributed to his failing health. He fasted once a month in penitence for Peter Hawkins's death, paid the gamekeeper's widow £20 every year and left her the same amount in his will. The king died on 27 March 1625, and the following year the archbishop crowned the new king, Charles I. But in the new reign Abbot played little part in court or church affairs – although he continued to show an interest in his foundations in Guildford, despite spending little time there. His health continued to deteriorate, and he died, aged 72, at his palace in Croydon on 4 August 1633. Abbot's will, which he had drawn up the previous year, stated that he wished to be buried in Guildford 'in the same town where my flesh had the beginning'. His executors were his brother Sir Maurice, Lord Mayor of London, and Maurice's son. On 3 September his state funeral began in Croydon. Archbishop Laud, who succeeded him, was the chief mourner. His body was transported to Guildford where it was received the following day by the mayor. The High Street was draped in black and crowds of townspeople

Both reproduced by permission of Surrey History Centre.

43 *Holy Trinity Church, 1888.*

followed the coffin to its final resting place, where the funeral oration was given by John Bowle, the Bishop of Rochester. Abbot was buried in Holy Trinity Church opposite the Hospital of the Blessed Trinity that he had founded, in a Renassiance tomb commissioned by Sir Maurice Abbot as a memorial to his famous brother. John and Mathias Christmas, London sculptors, carried out the work and it was completed in 1635.

James II ascended the throne in 1685. He made no secret of the fact that he had embraced the Roman Catholic faith, and this did not make him popular with the English Protestants; they had not forgotten the difficulties caused by the plotting Roman Catholics. His brother

44 *Interior of Holy Trinity.*

Charles, while king, had sent James abroad for his safety, but Charles was adamant that his brother should succeed him as king. He did so on Charles's death in 1685. James still believed in the divine right of kings in spite of what had happened to his father, another strong believer in the idea. He was a very unpopular king.

Six months after James's arrival on the throne, the Duke of Monmouth, an illegitimate son of Charles II and a Protestant, determined to wrest the crown from his Roman Catholic uncle. When he landed in England with an army, Protestants welcomed him and he was proclaimed king in Taunton. But his rebellion was short lived; James had no intention of relinquishing his throne. A bloody battle was fought at Sedgemoor, the rebels were crushed and Monmouth was captured. He pleaded for his life, but James refused a pardon and condemned his nephew to death. Monmouth was escorted to the Tower of London under armed guard, and spent the night of 12 July 1685 at Guildford, which was *en route*. The most secure place to house a dangerous prisoner was the strongroom in Abbot's Hospital, a suitable cell for a traitor on his way to execution. Thereafter the room became known as the Monmouth Room.

James put down the uprising with incredible cruelty. The trials that followed became known as the Bloody Assizes, and were presided over by the infamous Judge Jeffreys. In an attempt to establish his unquestioned authority, James revoked all previous town charters and announced a new one, which gave him the power to dismiss any member of the corporation and impose his own nominees. This was exceedingly unpopular throughout the land, particularly in Guildford, but it remained in force for two years until, in an attempt to repair the damage he had done, James revoked it. But it was too late. Parliament was tired of him, and invited the Protestant William of Orange, who had married James's daughter Mary, to lead a revolution against him. When, in November 1688, William landed in Devon at the head of a strong army, men flocked to join him. James, realising that his days were numbered, fled to France, and the Protestant William and Mary ascended the throne.

FOUR

The Eighteenth Century

The turn of the century saw more improvements to Guildford's mills. In 1701 William Yarnold, an engineer, obtained a grant from the Mayor and Approved Men to set up a water company. Pumps were installed in the fulling mills to supply the town with water. Hollow elm-log pipes led to a reservoir, from which water was distributed to the town. The wool trade had gradually decreased and in 1714, the year the first George ascended the throne, the fulling mill was converted to grind wheat. Buying and selling wheat was profitable, and the Wey Navigation enabled Guildford to build up a thriving business. In 1768 it was decided to rebuild the town mills, and by March 1770 the eastern part had been rebuilt using brick, while the western part was only repaired. The water wheels were upgraded to a more efficient type.

Nightwatchmen patrolled the town from 8 p.m. to 5 a.m. They were instructed to call out the time every hour and also to report on the weather. The townsfolk might not have been particularly pleased to be woken up in the middle of the night by the call 'Three o'clock and a cold frosty morning'.

On 9 July 1709 there was a public execution in Guildford. Christopher Slaughterford, who came from London, was accused of the murder of his fiancée, Jane Young. He always protested his innocence and accused one of his servants of the crime; he had already been acquitted at an earlier trial in Kingston. But at his second trial, in spite of a strong alibi, Slaughterford was convicted, with the prosecution's case based solely on circumstantial evidence. He was sentenced to be hanged, and on the day of his execution he wrote and signed a statement denying any knowledge of Jane's death:

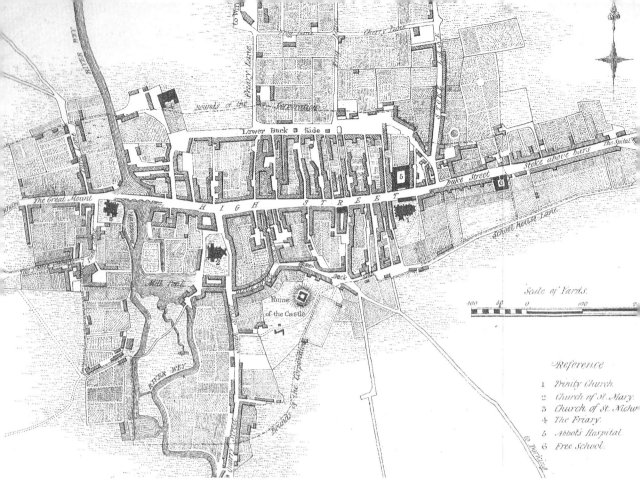

45   *Early map of Guildford (S. Grieg).*

Being brought here to die, according to the sentence passed upon me at the Queen's-Bench bar, for a crime of which I am wholly innocent, I thought myself obliged to let the world know, that they may not reflect on my friends and relations, whom I have left behind me much troubled for my fatal end, that I know nothing of the death of Jane Young, nor how she came by her death, directly or indirectly, though some have been pleased to cast reflections on me. However, I freely forgive all my enemies, and pray to God to give them a due sense of their errors, and in his due time to bring the truth to light. In the mean time, I beg everyone to forbear reflecting on my dear mother, or any of my relations, for my unjust and unhappy fall, since what I have here set down is truth, and nothing but the truth, as I expect salvation at the hands of almighty God.[1]

Because of the general lawlessness of the streets, an important act was passed in Parliament in 1715. This was the Riot Act, and it was aimed at preventing civil disorder: it could be read when there were gatherings of 12 or more. After its reading a notice was posted announcing that 'The Riot Act has been read', and the 'gatherers' had an hour in which to disperse. If they did not do so, the authorities could use force to break them up. The punishments for resisting were very severe: anyone who failed to disperse after it was read could be arrested, while anyone who resisted arrest or failed to disperse when ordered to do so could be wounded or even killed. It proved very effective, and Guildford made good use of the Act in the following century.

During this time the roads were greatly improved. In 1749 a turnpike was put on the Portsmouth road south of Guildford, which meant it became privately owned, and tolls were charged to use it. These went towards improving the road surface, and making it suitable for coaches: a stage-coach was now able to travel from Portsmouth to London in nine hours. Horses were changed after about 10 miles, but travellers still took the opportunity to stay at Guildford's popular coaching inns. Some of those who did not break their journey were sailors whose ships had docked at Portsmouth. They often spent their wages on hiring a coach to take them to London and the 'bright lights', and could be seen shouting and waving flags as their vehicle thundered through the town. Later, many of them might be seen walking back to Portsmouth, having spent all their money.

46   *View of the front of the new public buildings, including Tunsgate.*

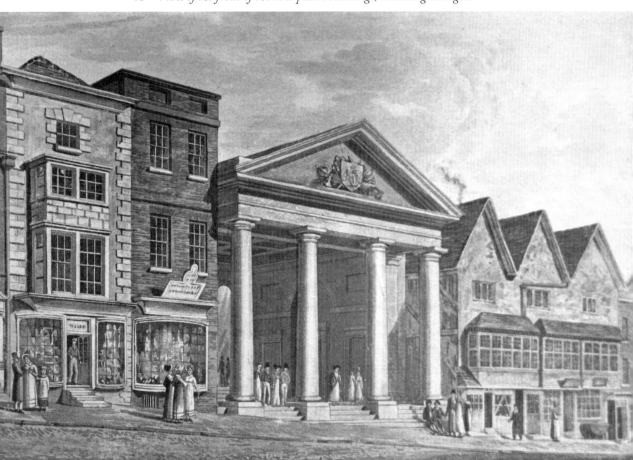

By 1784 the Royal Mail was also sent by coach; previously it had been carried on ponies by boys. Another transport innovation was the dredging of the ancient ford at Guildford in 1760 so that barges could travel upstream on the Wey Navigation.

It was not only the roads that needed repair; Holy Trinity Church at the top of the High Street was also giving cause for concern. By the 18th century it was several hundred years old. It is not known whether it was a Norman church or perhaps built in a later century, but the first rector was recorded in 1304. Manning suggests that it might have been build by the Testard family for the use of their tenants.[2] In about 1739 the church was repaired at a cost of about £750. The builders 'improved it by taking away the arches and pillars which supported the steeple'. This was not a good idea: 'the consequence was soon observed by the decay of the steeple and on 23 April 1740 the Tower of this ancient church fell down – whereby the whole structure, already gone to decay, was so much damaged that it became necessary to take it down and rebuild it'.[3] Archbishop Abbot's tomb had remained largely unscathed as it had been underneath an arch. It was moved for safekeeping to Abbot's Hospital, and later re-erected in a corner of the church. As most of the building had been destroyed when the steeple collapsed, a fundraising appeal was launched, but the money was slow in coming and it was not until August 1749 that the foundation stone for the rebuilt church could be laid. As there were still insufficient funds, some church land was sold. Even this did not meet the need, so for the next 14 years progress was very slow, and it was not until 18 September 1763 that the first service was held in the rebuilt Holy Trinity Church. The erection of the tower proved a temptation for one young boy who climbed up the brickwork. When he returned to *terra firma* his father was waiting for him, and administered a sound beating for his son's misdemeanour.[4] Father and son were both named John Russell, and they both achieved fame – the father as a local historian and four times mayor, and the son as a renowned portrait painter.

John Russell junior, who had climbed to fame, was born in Guildford on 29 March 1745. He trained under the Royal Academician Francis Cotes, who was a pioneer of English pastel painting. After Cotes's death Russell 'enjoyed the reputation of being the first artist in crayon-painting, in which he particularly excelled in the delineation of female beauty'.[5] By 1767 he had his own studio and in 1770 he won the gold medal for figure drawing at the Royal Academy School of Art. Russell travelled around the country undertaking commissions for portraits and miniatures. He painted in oils

47 *Town Mill, c.18th century.*

48 *Town Mill, c.19th century.*

49   *Holy Trinity Church and graveyard.*

and watercolours, but he became most famous for his works in crayon. He created his own crayons and developed a technique known as 'sweetening': this consisted of blending the colours in with his fingers and softening the outlines until they merged into one another.[6] In 1772 he published *Elements of Painting with Crayons*. His fame spread and he acquired more prestigious clients. During his lifetime he had 330 of his works exhibited at the Royal Academy and he became a full academician in 1788.

One of Russell's most important commissions came in 1789 when he painted a portrait of Francis Willis, the royal physician to George III. The king liked his work, and in 1790 the artist was appointed 'crayon painter' to the Royal Household. Russell painted the king, Queen Charlotte and the Prince of Wales. The Guildford House of Art Gallery in the High Street holds a large collection of his work, and some also hang in the Guildhall. Among the latter is one of his father. John Russell junior died in 1806.

Perhaps one of the most flamboyant Guildfordians of the 18th century was James Price, a chemist and alchemist. He was born James Higginbottom in London in 1852, but was left a legacy by a relative who stipulated that he should change his name to Price. James was happy to oblige. He went on to have a brilliant career at Oxford University, and at 25 he was awarded the degree of

Master of Arts. He was fascinated by chemistry, and in 1778 he became a Doctor of Medicine as a result of his work in that field.

Like many alchemists before him, Price was convinced he could create gold from base metals. He had a laboratory in Guildford where he worked on his experiments, and in 1781 he became a member of the Royal Society. When he created a red powder to which he added a mixture of base metals, stirring it with an iron rod, he was convinced that the resulting mixture would produce gold. So certain was Price of success that he invited a number of influential citizens to a number of public demonstrations, the last being on 25 May 1782. One of those who witnessed this creation of 'gold' was the historian John Russell. Price presented a sample of his 'gold' to King George III, and published the result of his experiments to great acclaim.[7] However, he did not convince the Fellows of the prestigious Royal Society, and they invited Price to perform his experiments in front of their members. While he had been happy to show off his experiments to groups of selected individuals, he did not show the same enthusiasm to do the same in front of the top chemists in the land. He made a number of excuses: he had no more powder and making more would cost money and damage his health; his method of producing gold was not economical; and so on.

The Society was not impressed, and insisted that he should repeat his experiments in London in front of their members. He was, after all, a member of the Society and if he did not comply he would bring dishonour upon it. Price arrogantly informed them that his reputation was above reproach, and he objected to having his work questioned – even by the Royal Society. Eventually, however, he was forced to bow to their wishes. When he returned to Guildford in January 1783, Price started to distil laurel water, which contained the dangerous poison prussic acid; he obviously had suicide in mind as he wrote his will soon afterwards. It was six months later, on 3 August, before he fulfilled his obligations and returned to London to demonstrate his experiment. But he did not do so. In front of the three members who turned up Price drank his prepared flask of laurel water. Shortly afterwards he was dead. It was a sad end for a man who had been a well-respected chemist and had been honoured for his research, but perhaps his flamboyant end reflected his character.

Another noteworthy citizen of Guildford, who certainly contributed more to the town than Price, was William Haydon. In 1756 he owned a draper's shop in the High Street where he sold cloth and specialised in foreign lace, which he imported. A successful businessman, he determined that the money he made should be kept secure, and he built himself a room in which he was able to lock up his valuables and keep them safe from any marauding vandals. Other people heard of his 'safe' room, and persuaded him to look after their money

50   *Haydon's Bank.*

and valuables as well. He charged them for the privilege, and soon realised that this new venture was more profitable than his old one. At first it was a sideline to his drapery business, but it gradually became more popular, and in 1765 William Haydon opened Guildford's first modern bank at 29 High Street. It flourished as more and more local people were willing to trust their money to him.

Guildford, along with other towns, continued to celebrate 5 November, but bonfires and fireworks were used at other times too. When Admiral Blakeney passed through Guildford in 1756, his success in the Seven Years' War was celebrated with fireworks and a bonfire. However, the celebrations sometimes erupted into violence and it was not always Guy Fawkes whose effigy was burnt; sometimes the effigy of an unpopular citizen who had offended the mob that year would be tossed on to the fire. Towards the end of the century the authorities became increasingly concerned about street mobs because of what was happening across the water in France. The French Revolution demonstrated the power of mob rule, and England had no intention of going the same way. Guildford banned the use of fireworks except to celebrate very special events. Bonfires were also banned, but this sometimes caused more problems as illicit bonfires were lit, which resulted in clashes between the crowd and the authorities.

The famous Guy Riots of the following century had their origin in the celebration of 5 November. It is likely that the Guy societies were formed at this time, to keep the tradition alive when the authorities started to ban bonfires.

In March 1739 Matthew Richardson, an enterprising accountant and surveyor, published the result of a mammoth project. This was his 'Ichnography' or 'Ground Plan of Guildford' – the first detailed survey of the town. In 1607 John Harris had engraved and published a rough plan, but it had been difficult to establish boundaries, particularly of common land – so it was not as detailed as the map attempted by Richardson. This latter was beautifully detailed, showing houses, green areas and roads. The size of the town seems to have changed little since medieval times.

This was not the only work Richardson produced for Guildford. In September of the same year he attempted something that had not been done since 1086, when William the Conqueror ordered his clerks to compile the Domesday Book. William had been interested in the amount of tax he could levy on his subjects, while Richardson was interested in the people of Guildford. After careful research he decided that 'according to the strictest computation this deponent has been able to make', 536 families resided in the area, making the population 2,574 in total. However, the accuracy of his findings is in doubt: he may not have taken into account the frequent visits to London made by many of the local residents, who often stayed in the capital. Although he dates his deposition as 28 September, he must have taken longer than that and some of his findings may have been from outside the actual town boundary. However, despite these shortcomings, Richardson is certainly to be congratulated on undertaking such a huge task at all.

The 18th century saw the appearance of a number of books and pamphlets about the history of Guildford and the surrounding area. In 1777 the first pamphlet about the history of Guildford was compiled by John Russell, the bookseller and historian mentioned above. John Russell senior was a well-known local figure, elected mayor of the town on four occasions. The first time was in 1779, two years after the appearance of his pamphlet, then in 1789, 1761 and for the last time in 1797. The second edition of his work, published in 1800, was more detailed, but unfortunately it was not carefully edited: a great deal of searching was required to find particular facts, as there appeared to be no systematic order. Russell also relied heavily on oral reports, which might not always have been accurate.

Another who was interested in local history was William Bray, a solicitor, who was born in 1736 in Shere, a delightful medieval village near Guildford. One of the first to realise that documenting day-to-day life in diary form would be of value, he started writing a diary in 1756 and continued it for a number of years. Sadly, it is not as detailed as one would like it to be, but it is nevertheless a valuable document about 18th-century Guildford. Bray was also an enthusiastic antiquary, and from 1803 to 1823 he was treasurer of the Society of Antiquaries. His family had been lords of the manor of Shere for centuries, and he was a wealthy man.

In 1767 Bray contacted Owen Manning, who was planning a county history of Surrey. Manning had been born in Northamptonshire in 1721. Educated at Queen's College, Cambridge, he was ordained in 1743. For eight years he was chaplain to the Bishop of Lincoln and in 1763 he became a rector in Godalming. While pursuing his duties conscientiously, he continued his academic work.

Like Bray, he was an antiquary and soon became interested in the history of the county in which he lived. He started collecting appropriate material and making notes, and when he heard from Bray he was delighted, inviting him to collaborate on a history of Surrey. The two men worked closely together, sometimes enlisting the help of other antiquaries in the area. One of these was Henry Hill, whose notes Bray used.

Sadly, Owen Manning died in 1801 before the work was completed, but Bray was persuaded to finish it. The first volume of *The History and Antiquities of the County of Surrey* was published in 1804. Two other volumes followed later, the last in 1814. It is perhaps one of the most detailed county histories ever compiled, a much more scholarly attempt than Russell's work and covering the whole of Surrey, not just Guildford. William Bray died in 1832.

During much of the 18th century most of the entertainment available to the public had been provided by the guilds. However, an enterprising citizen, Henry Thornton, decided that the time was right for an actual theatre to be established in the town. He acquired a small red-brick building in a side street, and in 1788 he was granted a licence to perform 'Plays, Farces and Interludes' in Guildford. The theatre could seat 400 people, and for the next 60 years it provided entertainment of various kinds for the citizens.

The 18th century did not neglect its poor. In the early 13th century a leper hospital, dedicated to the martyred Thomas Becket, had been built on the outskirts of the town. Structured like a monastery, it was run by a prior or master and catered for the poor, elderly and sick. A chaplain conducted regular services. St Thomas's Hospital eventually closed as a leper hospital when the dreaded disease died out. The building then became almshouses, and these continued to function in the 18th century. The building was not demolished until the early part of the 19th century.

Abbot's Hospital was still thriving, and in 1796 another hospital was founded. This was Parson's Hospital in Stoke Road, and its function was similar to that of Abbot's Hospital. It is likely that it, too, paid two of the sisters a small amount to care for the inmates.

FIVE

The Nineteenth Century

In 1739 Matthew Richardson had calculated that 2,574 'souls' resided in Guildford. At the beginning of the following century, in 1801, the first official census of the country's population since William the Conqueror's Domesday Book, was held. The population of Guildford was now 2,634, suggesting that it had only increased by 60 since Richardson's survey. The official census was probably more accurate than Richardson's but even this might not have been totally correct. It was not until the middle of the century when the railway appeared that the population increased greatly. Since the introduction of the turnpike, traffic had increased. Although it cost one guinea to travel inside a coach and 12s. 6d. to ride outside, about 200 passengers travelled through the town every day, using 28 different services.

During the early part of the century the streets of Guildford were lit by oil lamps fastened to the top of wooden poles, but this changed with the introduction of gas. In 1824 a gas company was established, and gradually gas lights replaced the traditional oil lamps. These continued to flourish until the end of the century, when electricity took over. An electricity supply company was formed in 1891, and five years later the electricity works was established in Onslow Street.

Traffic continued to increase, and because there was so much passing through the town it was decided to widen Quarry Street. To accomplish this, the chancel of St Mary's Church was shortened in 1825. An apocryphal story suggests that this was done at the request of George IV, so that there was room for his coach to pass easily along Quarry Street as he travelled from Windsor to Brighton to visit his famous Pavilion.

George died five years later, on 26 June 1830, and his brother, William IV, ascended the throne. The country was desperately hoping for some kind of reform to reorganise the unequal representation in Parliament. George had been resolutely opposed to this, but William was more liberal and was prepared to listen to those who felt that the parliamentary system was long overdue for change. There was a new articulate middle class who objected to the fact that hereditary landowners ruled the nation without reference to the majority of its citizens. They felt it was time for a thorough overhaul of the financial, economic and social structure of the country.

In Guildford law and order was still enforced by men whose offices originated in the Middle Ages, or even before. Two constables and their assistants, known as tithingmen, were appointed by the town council, and two night watchmen could also be sworn in as constables.[1] In 1831 an Act was passed that introduced 'Special Constables' 'For Amending the Laws Relative to the Appointment of Special Constables and for the Better Preservation of the Peace'.[2] They were appointed by Justices of the Peace. Any householder could be chosen, but some were exempt for various reasons, although in certain circumstances the Secretary of State could overrule the exemption. Constables had the same powers as the police, and they could be fined up to £5 if they did not carry out their duties satisfactorily. They were divided into small groups under captains, and could be enrolled for up to three months – although frequently it was considerably less. The bell in the town hall was rung to summon them in an emergency, and they were then deployed in strategic positions around the town. In Guildford they were particularly required during the 5 November celebrations, which often resulted in violence and came to be known as the Guy Riots. However, the constables, whose numbers varied from 50 to several hundred, were not always effective. Theirs was not a pleasant task, and Henry Peak, appointed one year as a Special, remembered in his *Recollections* 'the ordeal we had to pass through night after night parading the damp and dismal streets for hours'. They often had to be on duty from dusk until the small hours, and during the violent riots it was not only unpleasant but also dangerous. Some Specials performed their duties conscientiously – on some occasions perhaps too rigorously. One year an innocent commuter walking home from the station was accosted by 'two ill-mannerly ruffians who forcibly detained' him and demanded his business. When he asked why they wished to know, they said that as special constables they had the right 'to interrogate all men of a suspicious character'. The victim could not have been pleased by the description! Other Specials were less enthusiastic, and some did not even appear on duty when summoned, preferring to pay a fine. In 1852 one

Special complained that he had already done his 'duty' while others had not even been called. In 1853, 10 Specials were fined for not appearing, and some disappeared before they had completed their tour of duty.

In 1831 a Reform Bill was eventually passed by the House of Commons, but the House of Lords, with its hereditary peers feeling threatened by its sweeping changes, rejected it. Concerned that the country might be on the verge of revolution, the king stepped in, using his personal influence to persuade the noble lords that change was essential if the country was going to survive. The Reform Bill was finally passed in 1832. This gave the vote to many members of the middle classes who owned land and property. The working classes were resentful that they had not been included, but at least it was a move towards a slightly more equal society: prosperous tenant farmers, artisans and industrialists now shared government with the hereditary landowning class. In 1835 the Municipal Corporation Act went further, and local government was reformed. This directly affected Guildford. Every town was instructed to create a paid police force to maintain order. In 1836, to the annoyance of many who had been members of the tightly-knit Guild, a democratically elected borough council, the Mayor and Burgesses, replaced the Mayor and Approved Men. Instead of the guild dominating, there was now open politics: it was 'the undoubted right of every burgess to select for himself from the burgess role the names of those persons he would wish to be councillors of the town'.[3] However, in the first elections after the Act there was only one new face among the newly elected councillors.

One of the first acts of the new council was to reform the police force. In January 1836 the Guildford Watch Committee met for the first time and appointed four constables, who were paid £5 a year, three night constables, a watch-house keeper and a superintendent. In 1841 the force was cut down to just three men. The Metropolitan Police had been founded in 1829, and the Guildford force adopted their uniform of frock coats and top hats. Each policeman was allocated two pairs of shoes, a frock coat, two pairs of trousers, a greatcoat and a waterproof coat every year; local tailors made the frock coats and trousers. The uniforms indicated that they were a civilian force and not a military one. Working either from 6 a.m. to 8.30 p.m. or from 7 a.m. until 9.30 p.m. the police had breaks for meals and were expected to attend church services every Sunday in the morning and afternoon. As they were overworked and underpaid, the turnover was high, so the use of special constables was vitally important. In 1851 the local police force was amalgamated with the newly formed Surrey County Police. Their role changed as society changed and transport improved.

Other reforms also took place in the 1830s. The government became concerned about the poor, and in 1834 it passed the Poor Law Amendment Act. By this the authorities were instructed to set up a Poor Law Union, which was to be run by an annually elected Board of Guardians. It was not until 1836 that this was formally instituted in Guildford. The first guardians were elected on 11 April of that year and future elections were to be held annually on the first Thursday after 25 March. There were 226 Guardians representing 21 parishes in the area, and 'The first Meeting of the Board of Guardians of the Guildford Union [was] holden at the Council Chamber in Guildford on Tuesday the Twelfth of April one thousand eight hundred and thirty six'.[4] The minute books of the Board of Guardians from 1836 to 1838 were beautifully written in copperplate handwriting and bound in leather.

Guildford has always been concerned about its poor, and as well as Abbot's Hospital there were already three workhouses in the parishes of Holy Trinity, St Mary's and St Nicolas's. Each catered for about 20 inmates, but more was needed – and in 1836, in compliance with the new act, George Gilbert Scott and William Bonylthon Moffatt designed a new workhouse housing 300 inmates, at a cost of about £5,000. As well as accommodation wards it contained a chapel, porter's lodge, board-room, laundry, dining area and kitchen. At the rear of the building was an infirmary.

An interesting note in the Minutes of the Board of Guardians on 1 May 1836 stated 'that no relief be given to any able bodied paupers in the Guildford District of the Union from and after the fourth of June'. It was assumed able-bodied paupers could and should find work. It was also stated that 'a weekly meeting be held at the Guildford Workhouse every Saturday at Ten o Clock in the forenoon precisely'. The day books of the workhouse were regularly inspected, and detailed records and accounts of expenditure were meticulously kept. On 10 February 1837 there was an interesting letter from the Poor Law Commission Office in Somerset House, confirming 'that the allowance of Beer in the Workhouse unless by order of the Medical Officer is altogether illegal'. As the typewriter was not in general use until the 1870s, it is interesting that the minutes from 1838 until the workhouse closed in 1930 were typewritten.

By 1859 the population of Guildford had grown considerably, and the need for a hospital to serve the community was becoming greater. To fill the gap a small house in Quarry Street, now Olivio's Restaurant, was opened as a free dispensary and surgery. The plaque outside it reads: 'From 1859 to 1866 this building housed the Guildford Dispensary providing the medical care for the poor of the town and was the immediate forerunner of the Royal Surrey County Hospital.' The Guildford and West Surrey dispensary was entirely

51   *Royal Surrey County Hospital.*

supported by voluntary subscriptions, anyone who could afford it contributing what they could. It treated outpatients, but doctors would also visit 'those who lived within two miles of the Guildhall'.[5] During the first year more than a thousand patients were treated, indicating the great need for a hospital in the area. Plans for this were finally drawn up in 1862. Florence Nightingale, who had been so instrumental in improving medical care and facilities elsewhere, was consulted over the plans. Lord Onslow provided a site in Farnham Road, and in July 1863 the foundation stone was laid and work on the new hospital finally started. Prince Albert had died in 1861, and Queen Victoria was asked if the hospital could be a memorial to him, as when he had visited Guildford he had received a rapturous welcome. She agreed, and the Royal Surrey County Hospital opened on 27 April 1866, with two wards containing 60 beds. There was no National Health Service to fund it, so it was necessary to rely on voluntary contributions.

The wealthy of Guildford proved generous. Some benefactors donated 50 guineas or more, while others preferred to give 10 guineas or more on an annual basis. It was from among these benefactors that the court of governors was formed, and they elected the management committee to run the hospital. Accidents and emergencies were dealt with swiftly, but all other patients were required to produce a letter of recommendation from one of the benefactors

52 *Arrival of Prince Albert.*

before they could be admitted. Treatment was free, but money was always needed. As well as donations, collections and fundraising events were held. The hospital definitely provided a much-needed facility in the growing town.

During the first year of the hospital's existence about 250 in-patients and over 1,500 out-patients were treated, and 12 operations were performed. By the end of the century the numbers had risen to 1,000 in-patients and 3,000 out-patients. It was not long before the original building had to be extended, and this happened several times over the following years.

In 1870 the workhouse hospital was enlarged, and in 1880 an advertisement for a nurse to work there stated that she 'must be unmarried, or a widow without family, be able to read and write, be well acquainted with midwifery, and fully competent to take charge of the sick in the Infirmary'. Her salary would be £25 a year and she would have 'furnished apartments in the Workhouse'. There were more developments in the 1890s, when an area was set apart for those suffering from infectious diseases, and a married couples' block was introduced.[6] In 1893 a large casuals ward was built in Union Lane, now Warren Road, to house vagrants. In charge were a married couple known as the tramp master and the tramp mistress. In a past life they had probably been vagrants themselves, but were now employed by the workhouse. New admissions had to remove their clothes so they could be disinfected, and they were forced to take a bath. Once clean, they were provided with temporary clothes from the workhouse and given a meal and shelter for the night. The female sleeping cells were wider than the male cells, so that mothers could have their small children with them. The male block consisted not only of sleeping cells but also four stone-breaking cells, each with a metal grille attached to its window. In each of these cells was a large piece of stone: to pay for their lodging, the inmates had to break the stone into pieces small enough to pass through the grille. This was not popular with the local population because of the noise. Inmates also had to remove oakum (tarred fibres) from old pieces of rope with an implement called a spike. The ward became known as The Spike. This name has been retained, and today The Spike is a historical monument.

George Orwell sampled The Spike, and in his book *Down and Out in Paris and London* he gives a graphic description of it:

> It was a grim, smoky yellow cube of brick, standing in a corner of the workhouse grounds. With its rows of tiny, barred windows, and a high wall and iron gates separating it from the road, it looked much like a prison ... The spike consisted simply of a bathroom and lavatory, and, for the rest, long double rows of stone cells ... It was a bare, gloomy place of stone and whitewash, unwillingly clean, with a ... prisonish smell.[8]

He comments on his experience:

> When we had finished bathing, the porter tied our clothes in bundles and gave us workhouse shirts – grey cotton things of doubtful cleanliness, like abbreviated nightgowns. We were sent along to the cells at once, and presently the porter and the Tramp Major brought our supper across from the workhouse. Each man's ration was a half-pound wedge of bread smeared with margarine, and a pint of bitter sugarless cocoa in a tin with margarine, and a pint of bitter sugarless cocoa in a tin billy. Sitting on the floor, we wolfed this in five minutes and at about seven o'clock the cell doors were locked on the outside, to remain locked till eight in the morning.

To the amusement of his fellow inmates, Orwell was amazed to discover there were no beds and he was expected to sleep on the floor.[9]

Baker's School survived until 1731, when it disappeared for 30 years. In 1761 it was re-established with the aid of various donations as the Blue-Coat School, but it was not as successful as its predecessor. It staggered on for nearly a century until in 1856 funds from George Abbot's manufactory fund, Baker's Charity and remaining assets from the school were brought together to endow a new school to be housed in Abbot's old manufactory buildings. Archbishop

Abbot's School seemed a fitting name for it. The school flourished for the rest of the century, and even rejected a proposal in 1884 to merge with the Royal Grammar School. Sadly it deteriorated during the following century, and was finally closed in 1993. However, after the Second World War another George Abbot School was opened a few miles from Guildford, so the archbishop's name was not lost.

By 1860 Thornton's Theatre had gone out of business, and in 1889 it was finally demolished. But the theatrical tradition was not dead, although the standard of performance was poor. Performances, usually of a music hall variety, took place in a hall in North Street, but many felt that the low standard and poor facilities did not do justice to the growing town. Many complained about the lack of a proper theatre. There were arguments on both sides. It was only the rich who could afford to go to London to see a play, and as they would be funding it they might object to mixing with the working classes, who were also demanding to be entertained. One man who felt that the workers were just as entitled to entertainment as their social superiors was John Dennis, a local businessman, who pointed out that his workers were earning good wages and as they could afford to go to the theatre they had a perfect right to do so. But it was not until the middle of the following century that the town could boast of a 'proper' theatre.

The Dennis brothers, John and Raymond, who had come to live in Guildford from Devon, took note of the enthusiasm for bicycling, and in 1895 opened their Universal Athletics Store at 94 High Street; this specialised in bicycles. They made a good team: John was the businessman but it was Raymond who was the better cyclist, and he travelled around the country publicising their firm. The brothers were also fascinated by the fledgling motor industry, and before the end of the century they were also building motor vehicles. Both were adept at publicity in their home town, but it was John who had a coup when in 1898 he drove a motorised tricycle up the High Street at the 'furious speed' of 16 mph. He was fined £1, but he considered the publicity generated by his feat well worth the fine.

In 1896 two other brothers, Frank and Arthur Drummond, established an engineering business at Pink's Hill. They soon outgrew their cramped premises and moved to larger ones at Rydes Hill, where they produced machine tools. A best-seller was a four-inch model engineering lathe regularly used by the Royal Navy.[10]

Interest in local history continued, and in 1845 another history of Guildford was published. At first it was thought to be a later edition of John Russell's work as it appeared to have been published by the Russells. However, in 1904 this was proved to be incorrect by George Williamson, who discovered that 'the book ... was written for Messrs Russell by a Mr F. Laurence in 1842'. He explained:

> This fact, not hitherto known, is rendered certain by the autograph inscription in the copy of the book given in 1852 by the author to his friend Mr Parry, in which he has recorded the fact of his authorship and the date when he wrote the book. This volume is now in the writer's possession.[11]

This book was better ordered than Russell's work, and was also illustrated with vignettes by C.C. Pyne, who later became the drawing master at the Royal Grammar School. Laurence would have used Bray's and Manning's work to supplement his own research, and probably adapted some of Russell's original work.

During the early part of the 19th century the number of coaches travelling to Guildford greatly increased. At least 10 coaches a day carrying about two hundred passengers stopped at the various coaching inns in Guildford, so that horses and passengers could have some much-needed rest. Fresh horses would, of course, be used for the ongoing journey. Large stables at the top of North Street were often used by night coaches for the changing of the horse teams. In the 1820s the medieval stone bridge beside St Nicolas's Church was widened to enable coaches to travel across it more easily.

Reproduced by permission of Surrey History Centre.

53   *Guildford to London Coach 1775, Francis Sartorius.*

54 *The old Railway Station, 1840s.*

Things changed rapidly with the advent of the railway. This had reached Woking in 1838, the year after Queen Victoria came to the throne. Guildford had no intention of being left behind, but it was not until 1844 that an Act of Parliament provided permission for a branch line to be extended to Guildford from Woking. In May 1845 the first railway station was built at the western end of the town, and on 4 September 1845 there was 'a meeting of gentlemen desirous of establishing a line of railway from Reading via Guildford to Reigate'.[12]

The railway spelt the end for the coach trade. By 1839 only 18 coaches ran through Guildford. In 1842 the mail was sent by rail instead of coach, and coach services ceased altogether.[13] In the 1870s there was a mini-revival of coach travel, but only for pleasure. In 1875 a Captain Hargreaves introduced his *Rocket*, which he drove enthusiastically between London and Portsmouth. Walter Schoolbred's New Times Coach was more successful. Starting in 1879, it travelled from Piccadilly to Guildford, and continued its rounds until halted by the First World War.

Six

The Nineteenth Century Continued

After the coming of the railway in 1845, Guildford attracted more visitors, and a number of popular guides to the town were produced. So also were a number of other publications purporting to be memoirs or local history culled from earlier histories. The production of these was aided by the number of printing firms that had been set up in the town. The first of these was started by Joseph Billing, who bought a printing firm in Woking from Benjamin Bensley for £450 in 1843. There was only one printing press but others were soon introduced. Joseph Billing insisted on 'excellent workmanship', and this remained a principle throughout the life of the firm.

The firm flourished and produced a number of books over the years. By 1856 it had outgrown the Woking premises, and Billing decided to move to Guildford. For £1,850 he bought a stone warehouse from a Mr Arthur Pimm. This was situated on the Railway Esplanade near the station, and remained the site of the factory until well into the following century. Nearby Billing built himself a house, which he named Coverdale. Before long there were 10 printing presses operating, and in 1860 steam power was installed to speed up the production of the books. When they reached the age of 14, Joseph Billing introduced his sons to the business. Joseph Harrild, the elder, joined in 1859 and Robert Thomas, his younger brother, four years later. They both learned as much as they could about the printing business, and in 1875 their father made them partners in the firm. Harrild took over responsibility for the composing department, while his brother oversaw the machine room and foundry. In 1875 they both became partners in the firm.

A variety of books were printed; there were novels, educational books, general literature and books on religious and medical topics. Between 1,000 and 1,500 copies for each title were produced. One exception was perhaps the most famous book the company printed: *East Lynne*, the bestseller written by Mrs Henry Wood. One print-run alone for this title reached 15,000.

In his 1949 account of the factory, H.S. Billing notes that Robert Billing's order book for 1873 lists 196 titles printed between June and December of that year. More extensions to the factory were made in December of the following year and also in 1876, at a cost of £1,207 10s. 6d. In April 1880 a storehouse was bought and renovated for £615 15s. 1d. In 1882 Joseph Billing retired. He continued to live at Coverdale, and was always available to give advice to his sons, who were now running the company. Later, on 1 January 1897, Maurice Lacy was brought in as a partner. In 1899 yet another extension was needed and the county surveyor, Henry Peak, was commissioned to supervise a large addition to the printing press known as the jobbing room. More extensions were needed in the following century.[1]

A number of other printers appeared during the 19th century. Some of them printed anything for an appropriate fee, and 'vanity publishing' became popular as more memoirs and local guidebooks were produced. One of the most interesting of these was John Mason's *Guildford 1897*, which was privately printed. John Mason's story was that of a boy from a poor family reaching the top. His father wished him to take advantage of the education offered by the school established in the 16th century by Thomas Baker. However, it was made plain to Mr Mason by the trustees of the school that his son was not of the right class to attend their establishment. John Mason recorded in his book: 'I have reason to believe that [my father] was much hurt by the remarks of the Trustees that it was not intended for such men as him.'[2] In spite of a chequered beginning, John Mason justified his father's faith in him by becoming a prosperous builder, and in 1894 being elected mayor.

Another printer was Charles Biddle, who set up his printing works on the corner of Martyr Road and Haydon Place. While he started by merely printing short material, he later became a book publisher. Biddles remained in Guildford until 2004.

In 1854 the increasing interest in local history spurred a group of enthusiasts to form the Archaeological Society. Founded in Southwark, it was based in various London locations before it was decided, as with many other institutions in the 19th century, to search for a more permanent site outside London. Guildford was chosen, and in 1878 the Surrey Archaeological Society made its permanent home in a building close to Castle Arch at a nominal annual fee of £12. The public was to be allowed to view the artefacts that the society had collected.

In the mid-19th century there was a flurry of newspapers published in Guildford. Some of them lasted for only a brief period while others endured for longer. One of the titles that lasted was the *Surrey Advertiser*, which first appeared on 30 April 1864. Its first edition informed its readers that it would appear on the first Saturday of every month and would be 'circulated gratuitously among all Classes of the Community, and sent to upwards of 500 Hotels, Inns, Public institutions and coffee-rooms in Surrey, Hants, Sussex and Middlesex'.[3] The early editions contained several pages of advertisements – no doubt to pay for the 'gratuitous' circulation, but gradually more articles crept in. Eventually it was no longer a free paper but had to be bought. It continues to keep Guildford residents up to date with their town's news, as well as providing county news.

On 11 March 1834 the Guildford Mechanics Institute was founded for the 'promotion of useful knowledge among the working classes'. A meeting was held in Mr Whitburn's auction room in the High Street, and five individuals were appointed to set out the rules of the new Institute. Lectures were to be given, a library set up and a librarian appointed.[4] In November 1835 a Mr Crosskey offered the institute the use of two rooms at the back of his shop at a rent of six guineas a year. The lease was to run for three years, but the first six months were to be free so that any appropriate repairs to the building could be made. Before long, there was some disagreement among the members and a rival society, the Literary and Scientific Institute for Mechanics and Others, was formed on 2 February 1835.

55 *Guildford Institute.*

The two societies operated independently, but friction between them continued. Eventually, however, they decided to bury their differences because it was more economical to act as one group, and on 14 June 1843 they joined forces under the name of the Guildford Institute. All went smoothly until 1860, when some members considered the subscription too high for working men. Again a rival institution was set up, and it was not until 1892 that they were reunited. A new building was bought in Ward Street, and the Guildford Institute continues to provide lectures, a library and education services into the 21st century.

At first the railway benefited not Guildford itself but those wealthy men who worked in London for high salaries and liked the idea of a country residence in the pure air and tranquil atmosphere of a rural town. Perhaps they were influenced by *The Stranger's Guide to the Principal Objects of Interest in Guildford*, published in 1846 by G.W. and J. Russell. This stated that 'the most ancient Borough of Guildford, the county Town of Surrey is most advantageously and delightfully placed on the banks of the River Wey'.[5] It also extolled the beauty of the surrounding countryside: 'The picturesque and justly admired neighbourhood of Guildford owing to its great diversity of soil is peculiarly rich in botanical productions and will amply repay a visit from those who are interested in collecting and studying the beauties of nature in the native haunts.'[6]

A Handbook to Guildford by W. Stend, published in 1859 and reprinted in 1862, assured the reader that 'Guildford can vie with any town in the south of England in its railway communications.' After listing a variety of railway lines linked to the town, it concluded that they 'render Guildford an important centre, and a most convenient place from which any part may be reached'. The *Handbook*, 'embellished with engravings on wood from original drawings', also suggested 'Walks around the town' and described the 'Flora of the Neighbourhood'.[7]

The new residents established their families in newly built elegant mansions on the outskirts of Guildford. In 1870 yet more were enticed by the following advertisement: 'City men may find in the suburbs of Guildford elegant residences within an easy distance of their place of business.'[8] The ploy was successful, and the town played host to a number of new residents. In 1885 another line from Surbiton to Guildford via Cobham was opened. Over a thousand workmen were employed to build the new station, named London Road, on the eastern side of the town; a huge embankment connected it with the main station. Because of the new station, more attractive villas were built to house the wealthy on that side of the town. These cost between £3,000 and £5,000 to build, and some owners also erected several workmen's cottages for which they could charge rent. At first the new residents were not popular; their establishments had been built just outside the town, so local traders did not benefit from their custom. They 'daily drove to the station to go to London and, as a rule the majority of that class brought back with them all the necessaries of life from London instead of giving their support to the tradesmen of Guildford.'[9]

The cattle market, which had been held in the High Street for centuries, was now causing problems. Fastidious commuters objected to the smell and the dirtying of their shoes from the inevitable debris on the street. Farmers and traders voiced strong objections to moving it, but they were ignored, and in 1865 it was transferred to North Street. Much later, in 1896, it was moved even further away from the centre to Woodbridge Road.

With the influx of rich Londoners, the population of Guildford was increasing. Not only were professional men moving their families away from smoke-filled London, but there was also another type of new resident closely related to the earlier newcomers – wealthy retired men who had made their money and wanted to spend the autumn of their lives in more tranquil surroundings. With its frequent train services to London, Guildford was ideal both for those who were still working and those who, while retired, wanted to keep in touch with the outside world. A great number of these were retired army and navy officers.

Hooke's *Guide to Guildford* published in 1894 detailed excursions which could be made from Guildford by railway: 'Owing to the excellent railway

56   *River Wey.*

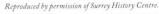

Reproduced by permission of Surrey History Centre.

Both reproduced by permission of Surrey History Centre.

57 & 58   *Railway station, c.1850.*

accommodation which Guildford possesses, the visitor has ample facility for making excursions to a number of interesting spots.' Among others, 'excursions may be made to Hampton Court, Windsor Castle, and Virginia Water, all within a sufficiently easy distance by rail to allow us to return to Guildford the same evening'.[10]

One of the most important new residents of Guildford to use the railway was Henry Peak. He chose to forsake the busyness of London and make his permanent home in Guildford. Born in London in 1832, he was the son of a gilder. 'I was born on Saturday the 18th of February at a quarter past six in the evening ... a troublous time it was too for England.'[11] He appears to have had a happy childhood, and enjoyed his school days:

> In 1844, much to my delight I was sent to a good school for boys. This was in Myddelton Street, Northampton Square, and conducted by Mr Charles Eves. Hitherto I had only been to Girls' Schools, carried on in ordinary rooms of private houses; but now the schoolroom was a large and lofty one, built for the purpose in the garden of the house. Upon entering the school, I was tried by the master as to my capabilities, and, as a result, was put into a class with boys, some of whom were much older than I, who was at the time about twelve. In arithmetic I was behind. In grammar also very deficient; but in reading, spelling, recitation and composition, of all of which I was fond, I was soon top of the class ... As to drawing, in which I had never had a lesson and for which extra my father was not prepared to pay, this being my natural bent, I excelled almost all the boys, and did for some of them the work which they were supposed to have performed themselves.[12]

The young Peak was soon in trouble for doing his classmates' drawing work for them but the master recognised his talent. So did his father:

> My good father, seeing plainly my natural bent as to drawing, in which I employed myself upon every possible opportunity ... rightly perceived that lithography, engraving or the like, would be occupations congenial to me, and that in them I might perhaps attain some proficiency; he therefore sought for me an entry into such an establishment ... [However he] was reluctantly compelled to abandon the idea, for he found in every case, the premium required would be beyond his means.[13]

Because of the fee required, Peak could not be apprenticed to any trade or profession. He eventually found work with a printer and enjoyed it, although it was not what he had hoped to do: 'I liked the beginning of the active life at Mr Howell's very well and strove to learn and make myself useful, believing that I have now entered upon the occupation which was to be that of my future career'.[13] However, in spite of his lack of formal training, he taught himself the craft of an architect and eventually became one of the most prolific architects of the 19th century. As he wrote later:

> I have had to gain my own livelihood from an early age [but] I have sought self-culture and, feeling my deficiencies, have constantly longed for more knowledge and wisdom and it seems wonderful to me that, in pursuing the profession of an Architect and Surveyor ... I should have been able to acquire sufficient knowledge to practise the same with at least *some* measure of success.[15]

Through a local contact, Peak was offered a job in Guildford as an assistant to a prosperous builder, Moss, who had his office on the Portsmouth Road. Peak was 19 when on 10 February 1851 he travelled the 30 miles to Guildford on the train to take up his new post. He was greatly impressed with the railway:

> What a marvellous development there has been since my boyhood, of the Railway system. People who now journey so quickly and easily to their desired destination, even in *third* class carriages ... can scarcely imagine the improvement that has taken place, as regards speed, comfort and convenience, compared with the unpleasantness of similar travelling less than fifty years ago.[16]

Peak described his new employer as

> a short, fat, bald, bespectacled man aged about 58. He was *not* a man of much education but quick and determined of purpose – a terror to builders. Neither was he a draughtsman or architect in the proper acceptance of the term, but he possessed great practical knowledge.[17]

His employer's wife helped him to find lodgings in Commercial Road with a Mrs Nye. Peak learnt a lot from his employer, and also continued rigorously with his own studies. He lived frugally and saved as much of his meagre wages as he could. Also living there was Miss Dalman, Mrs Nye's niece. When her parents died, Mrs Nye had adopted her and she had come to live with her aunt in Guildford. Now grown up, she ran a school – and Henry Peak fell in love with her. They were married in London on 17 June 1856 and returned immediately to the small rented house in Stoke Fields. Mrs Nye moved in with them, and Mrs Peak left teaching to help her husband with his work. In 1858 the Peaks moved into a larger house in Commercial Road opposite Mrs Nye's old house. Peak adapted one of the rooms for an office, but later he rented a larger office in a house in Market Street. He worked for Moss for seven years, but then misfortune struck his employer: he speculated in a building venture and lost heavily. His business failed, and Peak had to decide whether to find another employer or start up on his own. He chose the latter.

But, just as John Aylward had found in a previous century, it was not easy for a 'foreigner' to set up a business in the closely knit town. Peak noted that the 'practice of tradesmen and others of Guildford and Godalming of meeting in a social way at hotels and discussing business' was prevalent. But he was 'not without friends' who promised 'to introduce [him] to those who would put work in [his] way'. However, Peak declined all invitations and decided to set up on his own – a brave move that was to prove very successful.

In 1862 Thomas Sells, a local doctor, commissioned Peak to design a brand-new suburb to the east of the town in the parish of Holy Trinity Church. It was to cater both for the rich and the poor: there were to be impressive villas costing at least £5,000 but also small cottages that could be rented for a few shillings a week. It was an ambitious project, and probably the first of its kind in the country. The roads were all named after famous medical practitioners, and Sells named the area Charlotteville after his wife. It was self-sufficient, as it contained a school, several shops, three public houses and a small chapel. This was known affectionately as the tin tabernacle: constructed of green corrugated iron, it sat amid the splendour of the surrounding countryside. It was the centre of the community, and was only demolished in 1967. The community itself survived until the Second World War, and today Charlotteville is a conservation area.

In 1864 Peak became the first borough surveyor, a post he held for the next 28 years. This came with a salary of £10 a year, which he noted in his *Recollections* was 'a nominal amount, until it was explained what duties I had to carry out'. He had arrived in Guildford at the right time. The town was emerging from its medieval past and looking to the future, and Henry Peak was the man who created a modern town; much of his work is still evident today. His salary was eventually increased to £100, but he was frequently out of pocket as he often financed his own schemes.

In 1872 Peak designed a new brick fire station. In the early 19th century fire precautions were sadly lacking. The two fire engines stored at the town hall and at Tunsgate were operated by local blacksmiths; one of these engines could not travel more than five miles from Guildford without the permission of the mayor. To make life even more difficult, the engines, buckets and ladders were not all stored in the same place, and when they had finally been assembled a supply of water had to be found. This was not always easy, as the water mains were turned off at night to prevent leaky pipes causing flooding. When in June 1851 a shop fire had needed water, the landlord of the *George Inn* had provided the tank of water stored in his yard. It was not until 1863 that a volunteer fire brigade was formed, and a shed in North Street was built to house the newly purchased horse-drawn fire engine. Henry Peak's brick fire station paved the way for a professional fire service, which was operational by the end of the century.

Other commissions followed: Peak built churches, villas, roads, bridges and cemeteries, creating a Victorian town to be proud of. One of his most enduring projects is Guildford's High Street. In the 1860s he replaced the uneven medieval street with granite sets – the cobbled street that is still there today. It cost £12,000, which necessitated borrowing money, but Peak noted that he 'did not receive a penny above [his] bare salary'.

Peak's most controversial work was the building of a bridge commissioned by the Earl of Onslow. As it was to be on his land, he agreed to pay for some of it, but he required the Corporation to contribute £6,500. The High Street traders objected because they thought it would damage their trade, and they were not happy to foot the bill for a noble lord's fancy. They were overruled, however, and the bridge was duly built, opening in July 1882. The traders showed their annoyance by circulating a poster:

59 *Fire station.*

60   *High Street.*

OPENING OF THE NEW BRIDGE

Rejoice O ye ratepayers
That £6,500 of your money has gone to oblige a Noble Lord
Rejoice O ye tradesmen
That it is not spent in the town, but at the Civil Service Stores.
Therefore shut up your shops and be merry, saith the Mayor.[18]

During the 1880s the borough council bought several sites to be used for the public's leisure time. In 1885 they acquired the castle grounds surrounding the ruined keep. Henry Peak was invited to plan a pleasure park, and this was opened to the public in 1888. At the entrance to the nearby bowling green an elegant stone column provided the first gaslight stand in the town. A major feature of the new recreation ground was a pond in which both fish and mallards swam. Recently it has been refurbished by the borough council in partnership with the Guildford Society. In 1889 Stoke Recreation Ground was purchased, and in the same year one of the first public swimming baths in the country was opened in Castle Street.

The council was determined that Guildford should keep up with modern trends. From 1885 domestic refuse was regularly collected by horse-drawn carts, which were based in the council's depot in Bedford Road; the same year Clive Road saw the first council houses appear, and between 1889 and 1895 an advanced major sewerage scheme was introduced.

Peak was not really a political animal, but he was persuaded to enter local politics and in 1899 he crowned his career by being elected mayor. He was not happy, however, about the lavish banquet and drinking bout paid for by the mayor that always followed the inauguration. This supported the class system: no poor man could be elected mayor as he would not be able to afford his high office. By the time Peak became mayor he could presumably be classed as wealthy, although much of his own money had been used to finance his projects.

Although Guildford was not normally a violent city, the reforms of the 1830s stimulated resentment among some of the citizens. One of the first acts of the newly elected council after the Reform Act was to organise a borough police force to control the rioting. This usually reached its peak on 5 November, when the Guildford Guys lit a bonfire in the High Street opposite Holy Trinity Church. Elections always took place in November, so the resulting rioting usually had its roots in political resentment, and anyone who had offended the mob during the year could expect to be targeted on 5 November. While still in London Henry Peak had heard of the infamous Guildford Guy Riots: 'I had, of course, heard something of the lively doings which might

61   *Horse-drawn dustcart.*

be expected and in London ... there were celebrations ... but they were in a very tame and small way, in comparison with the doings at Guildford.'[19] The Guy Riots grew increasingly violent over the years. The Guys were usually disguised in grotesque carnival costumes, which effectively hid their identity, and they were organised with military precision. Their eerie rallying call, the 'Phillahoo Muster', was heard at dusk on 5 November, and this was the signal for all law-abiding citizens to barricade themselves in their houses. As wooden shutters were greatly in demand, a number of builders and carpenters profited from the riots, but most citizens were furious at the wanton damage caused, the ineffectiveness of the police and the poor reputation of the town that was gained. Henry Peak has left a dramatic account in his *Recollections* of the riot he witnessed in November 1852:

> I left my office rather late in the evening to go to my lodgings, and upon crossing the Bridge an imposing spectacle presented itself. There in the distance at the steps in the roadway opposite Trinity Churchyard a great fire was burning, brilliantly lighting up all around, and the whole town was as if in a state of siege. Every shop window not protected by shutters was barricaded, and wet straw and manure heaped over the areas and gratings ... to prevent the penetration of fireworks. These were formidable and dangerous things, being immense squibs many of them 12 or 15 inches in length and 1½ to 2 inches in diameter, and being chiefly loaded with gunpowder and heavily rammed, their force of explosion when discharged was tremendous and notwithstanding the precautions taken, I saw several mount to a great height and some actually entered the upper windows of houses. Curiosity drew me to the bonfire where a great and lawless crowd was gathered, the chiefs, fantastically dressed, were members of the Guys' Society, an organised body defying the police and officials of the town and a saturnalia of mob rule was being carried on. The whole place was at the mercy of the Guys, who gave orders by means of a horn.[20]

It was during this year that official complaints were made about the damage caused by the Guys. Both came from clergymen. The Rev. Mr Shrubb complained that the rioters attacked his premises and stole some palings from the oak fence surrounding his garden. He said that for two or three hours 'they were employed in their outrageous proceedings'. He described the town as being 'in a state of complete riot with no one to oppose their lawless proceedings'. It only ended when 'the men themselves [were] exhausted and worn out'.

Both Shrubb and another clergyman, the Rev. Mr Walford, applied to the town authorities for compensation, but the borough bench was unsympathetic. No one, said the magistrates, had warned of the possibility of a riot, so precautions had not been taken. Unimpressed by this excuse, the victims complained to the Home Office, who demanded an explanation from the borough. The mayor,

62 *West Surrey Election, 29 September 1849.*

Mr Taylor, made the excuse that the rioters were not natives of Guildford, and suggested that keeping order was difficult as the national government did not give the town enough support. Unimpressed, the Home Office informed the mayor that if he could not maintain order in his town using the civil authorities then he should ask for help from the military. The riots continued in subsequent years.[21] One of the worst occurred in 1854. A new bonfire was lit in Mount Street, and groups of thugs armed with vicious nail-studded clubs were stationed in various strategic positions around the town. As the police approached the bonfire, the mob charged out and completely overpowered them.

Over the next decade the situation grew worse, and in 1863 it marred what should have been a pleasant day. On 10 March the day dawned bright and clear. Guildford's streets were decorated with flags, and at six o'clock in the morning church bells joyfully rang out to celebrate the wedding day of the Prince of Wales to Princess Alexandra. By half past ten spectators were crowding the streets to watch the procession, which started from the *White Hart* at about half past eleven. The band of the 2nd Surrey Militia and the 13th Surrey Rifle Volunteers led the parade, while schoolchildren wearing rosettes and carrying flags and banners followed them. One school supported a wire frame, on which the Prince of Wales's feathers had been mounted using roses and laurel leaves. At the rear were the bands of the Union Workhouse and the 24th Surrey Rifle Volunteers. After parading around the town the children were treated to buns and a cold drink by courtesy of the 24th Surrey Rifles, while 300 elderly people sat down to a nourishing meal of roast beef followed by plum pudding washed down by beer. The meal, paid for by the public, cost 2s. each, and those who were too ill to attend were given the money in lieu. Before they ate, a choir sang 'God Bless the Prince of Wales', and when they had finished the National Anthem was played. At one o'clock there was a gun salute from the 24th Surrey Volunteers. The afternoon was occupied in games of various kinds and a football match was played in the High Street. There were frequent interruptions when the ball landed in the river at the bottom of the street.

An enjoyable day was had by all, but there was one bone of contention.[22] Unlike most other towns Guildford had decided not to have a bonfire to celebrate the royal wedding. This was a great mistake and proved costly to the town. Bonfires were always lit to celebrate great events and the Guys had no intention of letting such an important occasion pass without one. The *West Surrey Times* of 14 March 1863 agreed with them:

> Undoubtedly the committee who undertook the management of the Guildford Festivities committed a great mistake in not providing for a bonfire ... The consequence was what any sensible man might have expected. ... It was attempted to make Guildford unlike every other place in the county, by having no bonfire.

It continued by pointing out that it was unlikely that the 'loyal and conservative body who maintain old institutions ... were going to allow Guildford to be the only town in England without a bonfire on the wedding day of their future sovereign'.[23] The 'loyal and conservative body' were no doubt the 'Guys', and the paper was quite right. About 40 Guys were determined to show their patriotism. Wearing their usual grotesque costumes and carrying banners bearing the words 'God Bless the Princess Alexandra' and 'Long live the Queen', they headed for the top of the High Street and lit a bonfire in the usual place, opposite Holy Trinity Church. At first there was no problem but later, for some reason, 'they made a furious attack on Mr Eager's house'. Why this particular gentleman was singled out is not clear, but presumably he had offended the Guys at some time.

A few months later the Guys utilised another celebration day to cause havoc. This was during St Catherine's Fair, which was held every October. But it was before the actual fair, on Tap-up-Sunday, that the Guys were in evidence. The disturbance was so bad that it was even reported in *The Times* of 29 September 1863 to the great embarrassment of the town's law-abiding citizens. Apparently 700 young men – 'low characters of Guildford' – having taken full advantage of the availability of beer, converged on St Catherine's village intent on 'disturbing the peace'. They threw stones at those driving by, seriously injuring some, and encircled and attacked unwary pedestrians. When the police arrived, the situation was exacerbated; they eventually withdrew 'to leave the mob to their own course'. However, the constables placed themselves at strategic places around the village and prevented anyone else from entering the danger zone. The long account of the disturbance in *The Times* was followed the next day by a damning leader in the same paper criticising the authorities. It announced: 'The fault is entirely theirs for allowing the mob to get such head', and continued scathingly, 'If neither the borough nor the county police are able to keep the peace and secure the freedom of the highway it would be well if the Secretary of State for the Home Department were to take such steps as would remedy the evil, and at the same time make the ratepayers of the borough pay heavily for his assistance.'[24] Captain Hastings, chief constable of the Surrey Constabulary, reacted by writing to the Home Secretary to justify the behaviour of the authorities. He pointed out that 'no one as far as the police have been able to ascertain received any serious injury whatsoever' and described the affair as 'trivial and unimportant'. To cover himself, he added, 'In conclusion I beg to say that I have made arrangements for the preservation of the peace on Sunday next, in the event of any attempt being made to repeat a similar disturbance.'[25] The Home Secretary was not impressed, informing the superintendent that a more recent Act of Parliament prohibited the selling of beer without a licence, and that this negated the original charter. Hastings still tried to justify the tradition by pointing out that the selling of beer without a licence during the fair had been the custom 'for a great number of years'. However, he bowed to a higher authority and would 'give notice that the said practice will no longer be permitted'.[26] After the leader in *The Times* there was a flurry of letters from frustrated Guildford citizens to the Home Office pleading for 'special steps' to be taken to sort out the annual disturbances that brought the town into such disrepute. One irate gentleman pointed out that Englishmen living overseas were given 'such assistance and *protection* as may be necessary' by 'Her Britannic Majesty's Secretary of State', and that surely the same privilege should be enjoyed by those actually living in England!

After the trouble on Tap-up Sunday the fair itself turned out to be a 'very tame' affair, according to one local paper. It was raining, and at first there were few visitors. However, the stallholders did their best to liven things up. Outside a caravan announcing 'Manley's Museum of Science and Nature and

Art', Mrs Manley, a large middle-aged lady, danced enthusiastically as she beckoned customers inside to enjoy her conjuring tricks, 'all for the low charge of one penny'. Many had taken advantage of the relaxing of the licensing laws, and one entertainer playing a dulcimer was frequently hit on the head with a tambourine by his female partner to keep him awake. More visitors appeared in the evening. Most of them had also taken advantage of Tap-up Sunday and were definitely the worse for wear. However, most of them seemed good humoured and not bent on any mischief.[27] The day passed off calmly, unlike the previous Sunday.

Soon after this, Phillip Whittington Jacob was appointed mayor, and given unprecedented powers to bring the perpetrators to justice. Interestingly he was not a native of Guildford but had lived in the town for some time. A qualified surgeon, he was also a brilliant linguist and spoke a number of European languages as well as Persian, Hebrew and Hindustani. He was a sub-editor for Murray's *Oxford English Dictionary* on which he worked for several years, receiving praise for the amount of work he accomplished. Peak described him as 'a man of great force of character' – probably the reason why he was chosen to suppress the Guy Riots. He had been mayor when Peak had applied for the post of borough surveyor, and had originally voted against Peak's appointment. However, Jacob later admitted that he had been wrong and that Peak had been the right man for the job, congratulating him on the work he had done.

Jacob took his duties seriously. Late in the afternoon of 5 November 1863 he ordered troops to patrol the town until the early hours of the morning. Supporting them were the regular police and about 300 special constables armed with impressive batons. The troops remained until 21 November, when they were withdrawn. This, of course, was the signal for the Guys to appear again. At 11 o'clock on the evening of Saturday 21 November the 'hulluloo' rallying call of the Guys was heard in Stoke Road. About 20 grotesquely robed figures led a large crowd into the High Street where they hammered on the door of a magistrate, Mr Weale. Frustrated by the strong shutters, they turned their attention to the police station, and brutally beat up a policeman. Returning to Mr Weale's establishment, they smashed all the windows on the first floor and attacked several other nearby houses; one householder was knocked down when he tried to protest. Eventually the town hall bell was rung and about fifty special constables converged on the town. Jacob also rushed to the scene and read the Riot Act. The Guys removed their costumes and left them in the Union Workhouse before disappearing into the crowd which, cowed by the reading of the Riot Act, was dispersing. The special constables continued to patrol the town until Jacob dismissed them at about half past two in the morning.[28] A reward of £500 was offered for information leading to the arrest of the ringleaders, but none was forthcoming. No witnesses had ever come forward to name the Guys because of fear of reprisals. A local reporter, brave enough to write a detailed report of the riots, was threatened with death if he continued to do so.

The town pinned its hopes on Jacob's tough measures, and he was determined to dismantle the disruptive group. First of all he set about reorganising the police force. Since 1855 Vickers had been superintendent of the three policemen, but Jacob decided it was time for a change; he requested Captain Hastings from the Surrey Police to find a suitable replacement. John Henry Law was appointed, as were nine extra constables. Jacob agreed that Law should have the full support of both himself and the magistrates, and Law was installed in his new position by the end of November 1863.[29]

On 11 December the Watch Committee agreed to Law's request for six more policemen. This brought the numbers up to twelve. He armed them with cutlasses and drilled them rigorously. His discipline was strict. The town clerk was a little concerned about the cutlasses and felt that he should inform the Home Office about them, but Law got his way. The following November, Law and his men were prepared, and the riots were contained. Law noted that 'several attempts were made by the roughs to get into the town and commit their usual outrages, but their attempts were prevented'.[30]

On Boxing Day 1865 one of the most violent riots erupted. A policeman was severely beaten, and on this occasion his attackers were arrested. Four men were later charged with attempted murder. Three of them were found guilty and given lengthy prison sentences – the first time such a thing had happened. This encouraged more witnesses to come forward and identify many of the ringleaders. Hiding behind grotesque carnival masks, the majority of them were found to come from the upper classes, who had deeply resented the passing of the 1832 Reform Act as it had curtailed the power of the closely knit 'secret society' of the guild and introduced more democratic government.

Over the next few years resentment still flared occasionally, but law and order now prevailed and the citizens knew that rioters – whoever they were – would be brought to justice. On 5 November 1867, the year after Jacob retired as mayor, a grateful town presented him with the gift of a plate to commemorate his service to the town.

Until 1885 Guildford was one of only 38 boroughs that had the right to return two members to Parliament, and candidates had no reservations about resorting to bribery to secure their seats. At this time the ballot was not secret and the results of the poll and the voters were published, so who had voted for which candidate was public knowledge. Although Liberals were sometimes

63   *Alice and Sister by the river.*

64   *Alice through the Looking Glass (Jean Argent, 1990).*

returned to Parliament, Henry Peak noted that 'to be respectable or prosperous – to be *anything* at all, one must needs be Conservative or Tory as then more popularly called and I soon discovered that the ruling power of the town was almost entirely that way'. He even lost an important commission for restoring a church because one of the churchwardens was the defeated Tory candidate, who took revenge because Peak had not voted for him. Redistribution of seats in the Act of 1867 made the borough part of the county of Surrey, and Guildford lost one of its MPs. The Ballot Act of 1872 introduced the secret ballot, and bribery was eventually eliminated.

Another newcomer to Guildford who took advantage of the railway was Charles Lutwidge Dodgson – better known as Lewis Carroll. Born in Danesbury, Cheshire, in 1832, he was the second of 11 children. He was a brilliant mathematician and, after four years at Rugby School, he entered Christ Church College, Oxford, to study mathematics. When his mother died in 1851, his father, the Rev. Charles Dodgson, could not cope with such a large family on his own, so his wife's sister, Lucy Lutwidge, came to look after them. The eldest son continued to live in Oxford. He had matriculated in May 1850 and acquired a first-class degree in 1854. The following year he took up a post as mathematics lecturer at the college, and remained there until 1881. As the ancient rules of the university required that he take Holy Orders, he did so, reluctantly, in 1861.

Dodgson's earliest published works were on mathematical themes. His most famous book, *Alice in Wonderland*, was published in 1865 under the pseudonym Lewis Carroll. Although it was well known that he was Lewis Carroll, Dodgson himself never acknowledged the fact, preferring to hide his light under a bushel.

When his father died in 1868, the family had to leave the rectory in Croft, North Yorkshire, and find other accommodation. Although he was now living in Oxford, Charles, as the eldest son, was responsible for finding somewhere for his aunt and unmarried siblings to live. Guildford seemed a suitable choice. At the time it had a population of about nine thousand and was the county town of Surrey. It was popular with professional people, many of whom had retired there, and among their number were some of Dodgson's own friends. This might have influenced his decision. He was also no stranger to the railway and used it frequently, so this might also have been a contributory factor.

On 14 August 1868 Dodgson went house-hunting with an artist friend, Walter Anderson. He found The Chestnuts on what is now Castle Hill. Built

65   *The Rabbit and the Rabbit Hole.*

66   *Lewis Carroll's grave.*

in 1861, its name was derived from the line of chestnut trees that bordered its garden. A few days later his eldest sister Fanny, his brother William and his aunt Lucy also viewed the property, and approved of it. The family moved into their new home later that year. Dodgson continued to live in Oxford, but his six unmarried sisters made their home in Guildford until 1920, when the last remaining sister died. As they had rented the property, as was usual at the time, the property then reverted to the landlord.

Dodgson always spent Christmas at The Chestnuts, and often visited during other holiday periods. His family made a number of friends in Guildford, and many social events were held at the house. He often walked over the Hog's Back to Farnham, and it was on one such walk that the idea for the poem 'The Hunting of the Snark' occurred to him. It was in Guildford during his first Christmas vacation in 1868 that Dodgson finished the first chapter of *Through the Looking Glass*, on 12 January 1869, but he did not complete it until 4 January 1871, when he was also in Guildford. It was published the following year.

Dodgson had many friends, including a number of children. He made frequent visits to a Miss Edith Haydon who lived in Castle Gate, a house in the castle grounds. In 1990 Jean Argent, a student at the Guildford Adult Education Institute, created a beautiful realistic statue of Alice passing through the looking glass. It was presented to Guildford Borough Council by the Municipal General Insurance Ltd to mark the link between Lewis Carroll and Guildford. The statue now stands in the garden of Castle Gate.

Although ordained, it was rare for Dodgson to preach because he had a stammer, but in 1887 he was persuaded to preach in St Mary's Church in Guildford, and for the next 10 years he preached there once or twice a year. He made his usual Christmas visit to The Chestnuts in 1897, but while he was there he caught influenza, which affected his lungs. He died at the age of 65 on 14 January 1898. His simple funeral service was held at St Mary's by the Dean of Christ Church College, and afterwards his coffin, followed by the mourners, was carried to the Mount Cemetery, where he was buried.[31]

Haydon's Bank, which had been started by William Haydon in 1765, continued to be run by the family: his two sons, Thomas and Joseph, had joined him. William's grandson joined the firm in 1839, and in 1840 it started trading under a new name, Guildford Bank. But the business could not keep pace with the increasing demands made upon it, and in 1883 it was forced to sell to the Capital and Counties Bank. In 1899 the building was extended, but it retained its Georgian exterior.

SEVEN

The Twentieth Century

In 1901 another census was held. This showed that the population of Guildford had greatly increased, to nearly 16,000, since the census taken in the previous century; this was mainly because of the introduction of the railway. The first decade of the 20th century saw few changes in the town, but according to the *Official Guide of the Corporation of Guildford*, published by the Woodbridge Press, 'The estimated population at the Census of 1911 was 23,820'. This *Guide* stressed the advantages of living in the town, including a section entitled 'Why Guildford is healthy': 'Guildford has at least two of the most essential natural features of a healthy town, viz (1) It is situated on the declivity of a hill; (2) It is built almost entirely on the chalk.'[1]

The *Official Handbook of the Chamber of Trade – Guildford To-day*, published in 1912, gave a short description of Guildford's principal attractions 'illustrated from recent photographs'. A.D. Jenkins, the town clerk, stressed the great advantages the town had to offer.

> Guildford possesses, as a place of residence, an almost unique combination of advantages not in one respect merely but in several. (1) It was very healthy. (2) It had good sanitation. (3) The roads and footpaths are kept in good order and well lighted. (4) Police records show the borough is remarkably free from serious crime. (5) During the summer months concerts arranged by the Town Council take place in the picturesque Castle Grounds or in Rack's Close. (6) There are several recreation grounds.[2]

The population of Guildford continued to increase. In 1933 the town's boundaries were extended, causing a big leap in the number of residents.

67   *Aerial photo of Guildford Cathedral and surroundings.*

While there was some entertainment, there were still murmurings about the lack of a 'proper theatre' in the town. The wealthy could travel to London to see a show, but the majority could not afford to do so and bewailed the fact that there was nothing to do in the long dark evenings. However, there were some who felt that the town would not be able to finance a theatre. The theatre enthusiasts won the argument, and in 1912 the County and Borough Halls Company opened a theatre in North Street. This seated about a thousand people, and the performances enjoyed by the audience were of a much higher standard than those previously seen in the town. It flourished for 20 years, but then Surrey County Council introduced new licensing laws; to reach the new standards required, the theatre would need to raise about £20,000 for renovations. The Cooperative Society, which now owned the building, was unable to find the money, and in 1932 the theatre had to close. It remained in abeyance until after the Second World War.

Guildford has had its share of nat-  ural disasters as well as man-made ones. Because of the River Wey, the danger of flooding has always been present. The 20th century started with a flood when the river burst its banks on 15 February 1900. Timber from Moon's Timber Yard, which stood at the bottom of the High Street, was swept swiftly downriver to crash

GUILDFORD ST. NICOLAS FLOOD LEVEL 16 SEPTEMBER 1968

68 *Plaque showing flood level, 1968, about five feet above ground level.*

against the fragile medieval bridge, which collapsed under the onslaught. When the floods had died down, work began on a new bridge made of cast iron and steel. This was completed two years later in 1902. There were more floods in 1928 and again in 1968. On Sunday 15 September heavy rain fell continuously for the whole day, and in the evening the Wey burst its banks, causing considerable disruption in the town. St Nicolas's Church, beside it, was so low-lying that it was badly affected every time there was a flood. The congregation became resigned

69 *Floods in Friary Street, 3 January 1923.*

70 *Floods, 1968.*

71 *Wreck of old*
   wooden bridge.

72 *High Street flooded, 1900.*

73 *High Street flooded, 1900.*

74 *Floods, 16 February 1900, taken from bridge before it was demolished.*

75   *Floods by Yvonne Arnaud Theatre, 1968.*

to the persistent flooding, and in 1968 they even put up a plaque on the north wall of the church recording the flood level on 16 September of that year.

Man-made decisions also upset the town. In 1974 Parliament passed a Local Government Act, which heralded the end of the government system that, with a few variations, had existed in Guildford since Norman times. On Tuesday 26 March 1974 Bill Bellerby, who was the town's last mayor, handed over his seals of office to the chairman of the newly created Guildford District Council, which later became the borough council.

Guildford continued to expand. In 1970 the bridge near St Nicolas's Church was closed to traffic to enable building work to be carried out. Millbrook was constructed across the end of the High Street. More houses were built along the Downs despite vociferous protests from local residents. Family-run shops in the High Street were replaced with supermarkets and large chains, and eventually the High Street was pedestrianised. Traffic was diverted to Quarry Street, which had been widened in the 19th century (see p.67). In 1979 an SPCK bookshop was opened in the western bay of St Mary's church, remaining there until 1999.

In 1973 a property company acquired the *Bull's Head Inn* in the High Street, planning to transform it into a shoe shop. A petition signed by over 1,000 residents halted the company's plans for a while, and the building remained empty for two years until it was bought by a local businessman, who returned it to its original function. Sadly it closed as an inn early in the 21st century, and it was reborn as a jeweller's and later as a shoe shop.

Another site that caused considerable friction was that of the friary. This, after lengthy negotiations and many local protests, was eventually sold to a development company, which took seven years to build a huge shopping complex. The Friary Shopping Centre was opened in 1981, and two years later its roof deck was put to good use when County Sound, the local radio station, opened there in May 1983.

The iron bridge at the end of the town, rebuilt after the earlier floods, was later found to be unsafe and was dismantled in 1983. Two years later it was rebuilt, using the original stonework and the cast-iron side arches of the previous bridge.

The Dennis Brothers' motor vehicle business was so successful that at the 1903 show at Crystal Palace their sales figures beat all competitors. Their small workshop soon proved inadequate for the growing business, and a new factory was built in Onslow Street. These Robboro Buildings, as they came to be known, may have been the first purpose-built car factory in England. The business continued to expand, and in 1905 a new factory was established

76 *High Street, early 20th century.*
Reproduced by permission of Surrey History Centre.

77 *Proclamation of Edward VII,*
31 January 1901.

at Woodbridge Hill, producing cars, lorries and buses. When the company acquired a contract to provide the London Fire Brigade with motorised fire engines, they abandoned the production of private cars and concentrated on commercial vehicles. The factory was extended at the beginning of the First World War, when a contract for 7,000 lorries was received from the army. In 1934 the company expanded again by purchasing 21 acres of nearby land on which to build houses to accommodate their workers. The Second World War saw the Dennis brothers producing Churchill tanks. The post-war years were not kind and the company declined, finally closing in 1981. The factory was demolished in 1986.

In 1908 a higher educational establishment was founded. This was the Guildford Technical Institute, which had its campus in Stoke Park; its first courses were in agriculture and horticulture. It was officially renamed the Guildford College of Technology at the start of the Second World War in 1939, and at the end of the 20th century it became the Guildford College of Further and Higher Education. The college's two campuses merged in 2003.

In 1939 the County School for Girls was established, but it was almost immediately taken over by the Red Cross and adapted as a hospital. After it returned to its original use as a grammar school a number of new buildings were added over the years, including a new teaching block and another gymnasium. In 1978 it became a mixed comprehensive school and retained its sixth form. In 1993, three years after the school became grant-maintained, a three-storey building named after a former chairman of the governors, Stanley Cobbett, was opened. The beginning of the 21st century saw the school becoming a foundation school, and since 2004 it has been a specialist music college.

In the second decade of the 20th century dramatic changes for the country were hovering in the wings. On the evening of Sunday 28 June 1914 the *Surrey Advertiser* received the following telegram: 'A Reuter's message says that the Archduke Francis Ferdinand of Austria and his wife were assassinated at Sarajevo today.'[3] At first little notice was taken of an event many miles away, but then rumours of war started. The mayor, Mr G.S. Odling Smee, started preparations.[4] All planned railway excursions were cancelled, and armed sentries appeared outside the North Street Post Office and the telephone exchange in Market Street. Things came to a head on Monday 3 August, with a royal proclamation posted at the Guildhall and other public places throughout the town. It read: 'His Majesty, the King, having been graciously pleased to order by proclamation that directions be given to the Army Council for embodying the Territorial Force; all men belonging to the said Force are required to report themselves immediately to their headquarters.'

78   *Royal Standard over Guildhall, 1957.*

The following day the 5th Battalion of the Queen's Royal West Surrey Regiment, stationed at Stoughton, paraded through Guildford. There was an air of tense expectation everywhere while people waited for further news. They did not have long to wait. At last the expected message was posted to cheers from the crowd: 'England has declared war on Germany.' Their enthusiasm would, no doubt, have waned had they been able to see into the future. But at the beginning patriotism reigned.

Men rushed to enlist, and Col. J.W. Wray was appointed as a recruiting officer. Nearly 2,000 men had enlisted by 5 September and 140 National Reservationists had been called up. In July the following year all those between the ages of 15 and 65 who were not in uniform had to be registered by Guildford Borough Council, and local tribunals were set up to deal with conscientious objectors. The volunteers who had been accepted after medical examinations marched through the town to cheers from the crowd. The mayor, the town clerk and rectors from the local churches were there to see them off.

Special constables volunteered to take the places of police who had been called up, and civilian sentries were posted to guard the bridges around Guildford.[5] Even the High Sheriff of Surrey and the Earl of Onslow were among the volunteers. Some of the sentries proved over-enthusiastic, and there were several incidents of 'spies' being arrested; they were usually found to be citizens going about their lawful business. The special constables were eventually disbanded at a special parade in April 1915.

As well as men, horses were in demand, and many from the surrounding area were 'volunteered' by their owners, who were recompensed by the sum of 5s. for each horse. The purchasing officer was a Mr J. Hutchinson Driver of Woking.[6]

One result of the rumours of war was the panic-buying of food. There were early morning queues in the High Street outside the various food shops as members of all classes waited to buy – they hoped – the necessities of life. There was great annoyance in April 1916 when bakers announced that they had no ingredients to make hot cross buns. The same happened for the next two years, but by then the population had become resigned to shortages of all foodstuffs. To help with the situation, a Miss Ethel Cleasby, an artist who had had her work exhibited at the Royal Academy, came up with an idea. She decided to set up a Guildford Communal Kitchen, which would be open to all. It was established at the Ward Street Hall and could accommodate 50 people. Cooking apparatus and utensils were either borrowed or purchased, and diners were expected to provide their own crockery and cutlery.[7] A number of ladies volunteered to help, and Miss Cleasby supervised it. The Guildford National Kitchen was officially opened by Mayor Shawcross on 13 November 1917 and proved a great success. Its customers were mainly children, among whom were pupils from the Royal Grammar School. Because of the shortage of meat, some days were known as 'vegetarian days'.

The year 1918 saw 'sold out' notices appear on the doors of all Guildford's butchers, and Sunday 7 January that year was named 'Jointless Sunday'. It was not until 25 February the same year, when the war had only a few more months to run, that rationing for meat, butter and margarine was introduced. All Guildford citizens were issued with a ration book; they had to register with a particular butcher for their weekly meat ration and a grocer for butter and margarine. This made queueing for those items no longer necessary.

Khaki became the predominant colour on the streets as hundreds of troops were billeted in Guildford, and others flooded in to enjoy the entertainment that was on offer. Pubs were popular venues for the soldiers, but at certain times of the day they were banned from entering them. Drunkenness was frowned upon.[8]

It was not only healthy soldiers who were accommodated in the town. Soon after war was declared, the committee of the Royal Surrey County Hospital felt it had a duty to offer to care for the wounded. The 20 beds in Edward Ward were offered to the War Office, and it was also decided to enclose the nearby balcony and equip it with 10 more beds. The War Office accepted the offer. The first wounded arrived in Guildford on 15 October 1914, and the War Office contributed 3s. for each bed that was occupied. As noted above, the County School for Girls was adapted for use as a hospital at the beginning of 1915, and it catered for an additional 100 patients. The school was used as a Red Cross Annexe to the Royal Surrey County Hospital until the end of the war, when it reverted to its original use.

The citizens of Guildford had always been willing to help those less fortunate than themselves, and in September 1914 they showed their generosity once again. When the Germans occupied Belgium many Belgians fled, and when some refugees arrived in Guildford a Belgian Relief Committee was immediately formed. Clothes and food were provided and the town's residents welcomed the refugees into their homes.[9]

79 *Castle grounds with bowling green and war memorial.*

80 *War memorial.*

On 13 October 1915 the war came closer to Guildford. A Zeppelin was seen hovering over the town, obviously having lost its way *en route* to London. Ten bombs were dropped near St Catherine's; they fell in gardens or fields and the blast shattered a number of windows, but there were no human casualties. The livestock were not so lucky, as 17 fowls and a swan were killed in the attack.[10]

No more bombs fell on Guildford, but the town paid a heavy price as almost 500 men did not return home. Many had no known graves. When, on Monday 11 November 1918, the Armistice was signed and a notice was posted outside the *Surrey Advertiser* office, there was great relief. Flags appeared and the church bells pealed out their joyful message. On 25 January 1919 many soldiers returned to Guildford. They travelled by train and marched from the station through cheering crowds to the Guildhall. Here there was a reception to welcome them home.[11]

The official declaration of peace was read by the High Sheriff of Surrey, Mr J.H. Bridges, from the balcony at the Guildhall on the morning of 2 July 1919.[12] His grandfather, who had held the same office, read the same declaration at the end of the Napoleonic wars. The town crier, Mr Albany Peters, rang a silver peace bell, which had been presented by Harry Savage. Later the mayoress planted a peace oak tree in the castle grounds. It was not until 1925 that a war memorial was erected, also in the castle grounds, bearing the names of the 492 men who had made the ultimate sacrifice. The unveiling and dedication of this took place on Sunday 6 November in front of about 5,000 people.

By 1938 it was obvious that, yet again, war was a possibility. In view of the horrific use of mustard gas in the First World War, it was feared that it might be used again – not only on the soldiers but also possibly on civilians. The government decided that gas masks should be provided for every citizen and, to make sure that this could be implemented, a census was carried out. This showed that the population of Guildford stood at 42,000 people. Fortunately gas was not unleashed over the 'green and pleasant land' of England, but nevertheless citizens were required to carry their square brown cardboard boxes containing their gas masks at all times. Mickey Mouse masks were even provided for babies. Like all towns, Guildford again prepared for war. Units of the ARP, the Home Guard and the Auxiliary Fire Service were formed, and played their part during the following years. Emergency regulations issued by the government were implemented by the borough council.

When London was heavily bombed in 1941, many inhabitants fled the city for safer regions, and Guildford's population reached nearly fifty thousand. Although a number of bombs were dropped on the town, and many houses were damaged, no significant target was hit, and only four people were killed as a result of the bombs. One of the bombs was dropped on Charlotteville, as the pilot evidently mistook the hospital for a factory. Fortunately no one was injured. In 1944 a stray flying bomb landed on Stoke Recreation Ground, shattering windows in the surrounding area.

German bombs were not the only bombs in Guildford. Nearly 30 years later two more were detonated in Guildford after Irish resentment against the British government, which had simmered for centuries, flared up again in the 1970s. On Saturday 5 October 1974, at the height of the Troubles, the Provisional Irish Republican Army set their sights on Guildford, and they targeted two pubs that they knew were frequented by British Army personnel. That evening, at half past eight, the IRA detonated a six-pound gelignite bomb at the *Horse and Groom* in the High Street. A civilian, Paul Craig, was killed, as were two members of the Scots Guards and two members of the Women's Royal Army Corps; 65 other occupants of the pub were injured. The nearby *Seven Stars* pub was immediately evacuated, so when the second bomb exploded there were no serious injuries. The police immediately went into action, but it was not until three months later that they arrested three men and a woman. The trial took place the following year and the four, Gerry Conlon, Paul Hill, Patrick Armstrong and Carole Richardson, were found guilty in October 1975 and imprisoned.

They became known as the Guildford Four, and doubts about their convictions soon arose. However, they remained in prison for 15 years before a successful appeal was launched. It was eventually decided that they had made confessions under duress, and some evidence had been suppressed. They were later released, and no one else has ever been charged with the Guildford bombings.

With the increasing population after the war the council set itself the task of providing more amenities for its new residents. A public library had been opened in 1942 in the Old Borough Hall in North Street. It was not until 1962 that a new library was built near the top of the same street; today this contains a variety of books, magazines and research material and covers four floors. Another cultural innovation after the war was the founding of the Philharmonic Orchestra in 1945. Concerts were first held in the Odeon cinema and the technical college in Stoke Park, but in 1962 a new civic hall was built and this gave the orchestra a permanent home. The theatre also had a rebirth after the war ended, as the public was ready for some light-hearted entertainment after the deprivations of the war years. In 1945 two enterprising brothers, Roy and Patrick Henderson, were looking for a venue to introduce a new theatre, and Guildford, with its superb communications, was suggested to them. They promptly investigated, and found the town to their satisfaction. The new licensing regulations were still in force, but the brothers managed to find a way round them. They moved to Guildford and founded a theatre club, thus avoiding, at first, the crippling costs of building a new theatre. The public support for this was evident when, by the end of the month in which it was initiated, the club had enrolled 3,000 members.

In 1946 the Guildford Repertory Theatre was founded, performing for many years in the Borough Hall near the site of Thornton's original theatre. Many figures of national status in the wider theatrical world were involved in the productions. One of these was the actress Yvonne Arnaud, who lived in Guildford towards the end of her life. She was immensely popular not only in the town

81   *Yvonne Arnaud.*

but also in the rest of the country, and her support gave great credence to the fledgling theatre company. With many other residents, she was determined that Guildford would have its own theatre to reflect the growing sophistication of the town; sadly she did not see it in her lifetime.

1957 saw the 700th anniversary of the first charter granted to Guildford by Henry III in 1257, and the town decided to mark the celebration in style. It was decided to stage a pageant illustrating the town's fascinating history. At first Stoke Park was suggested as a possible venue, but it was eventually decided that Shalford Park on the south side of the town would be a better situation. The pageant was organised and directed by Christopher Ede with help from the curator of Guildford Museum, and crowds of townspeople took part.[13]

It opened with a Wey ferryman escorting a traveller along the Pilgrims' Way to Guildford, and the first scene was a re-enactment of the granting of the charter by Henry III. Other notable scenes followed: the sad funeral of young Prince Henry; the foundation of the Royal Grammar School in 1507; the dramatic accidental shooting of keeper Hawkins by Archbishop George Abbot. Boys from the Grammar School were shown playing cricket in 1551, while adults participated in the popular sport of bear-baiting. Another dramatic scene was when the Duke of Monmouth was brought to Guildford after his defeat at the battle of Sedgemoor. He was lodged in the strong room in Abbot's Hospital, which thereafter bore his name. 1845 saw the appearance of the railway and, of course, a re-enactment of a Guy riot was an obvious choice. The pageant ended with a reference to the new cathedral, which had not yet been completed but was seen as a 'symbol of faith in the future'.

82-4   *Queen's visit, 1957. She is standing on the balcony of the Guildhall. Photograph by Peter Ruck.*

Thursday 27 June was an important day for Guildford. The town was festooned with flags and streamers and crowds turned out to welcome the queen, who made a visit to the town to mark the anniversary. Before she arrived the bells of Holy Trinity Church rang out in her honour, and as she drove down the High Street they were joined by the bells of St Nicolas's and later by those of St Mary's. A loyal address of welcome to Her Majesty and the Duke of Edinburgh was read from the balcony of the Guildhall by the mayor. A portrait of the queen was commissioned by the Chamber of Commerce and presented to the town to celebrate the anniversary.

In 1958 Yvonne Arnaud died in Guildford – but she was not forgotten. Three years later, in 1961, an appeal of £200,000 was launched in her name to build a new theatre. The Guildford theatre project became national, and the launch of the appeal was held in the *Dorchester Hotel* in London. Many 'names' in the theatrical world were among the guests.

Within a year enough money had been raised to start building on the banks of the River Wey on the site of the old Millmead foundry. A member of one of England's most famous acting families, Vanessa Redgrave, was asked to make her mark before the building started. On the floor of the café a plaque on the floor states: 'Vanessa Redgrave stood on this spot on 18th September 1963 before the walls of this theatre had risen and the imprint of her foot marks its foundation.' The new theatre was to be named, appropriately, after another actress who had been so instrumental in its creation. The Yvonne Arnaud Theatre, which seated 568,

85   *Yvonne Arnaud Theatre.*

opened in June 1965 with a performance of Ivan Turgenev's play 'A Month in the Country', starring Ingrid Bergman. The 19th-century buildings adjacent to the theatre, which had once housed the town mill, were leased to the theatre in 1966 for use as workshops. Later they were reorganised, and a small intimate theatre named the Mill Theatre was created. The area was also used occasionally for art exhibitions.

86   *Mill Theatre.*

Another theatre was established in the 1990s. This was the Electric Theatre, which took over the building in St Nicolas Parish that had been vacated in 1968 by the local electricity company. The site was ideal for a theatre, and the building could easily be adapted. It was funded by Guildford Borough Council and donations were received from the public. The Electric Theatre put on its first performance in 1997 and it is now a major attraction in the town. It provides a venue for a youth theatre and for events in the Guildford Book Festival, held every October.

On the health side, the Royal Surrey County Hospital continued to fulfil demand and fundraising activities were increased. There were sales and bazaars and even an annual carnival procession. A number of voluntary organisations also provided care and comfort for the patients. During the First World War, while military casualties were treated, civilian care remained the same. Treatment became more expensive and it became necessary to charge both for out-patients and in-patients. To help those in need, a medical insurance scheme was introduced in 1928. This continued during the Second World War when, once again, military casualties were sent to the hospital. Demands on the hospital continued to grow: in 1947 nearly 4,000 out-patients were treated. Then in 1948, with the establishment of the National Health Service, it became the responsibility of the government through the taxpayer.

In 1930 the infirmary in Warren Road was acquired by Surrey County Council and renamed St Luke's. St Luke was the patron saint of doctors so this was appropriate; a nearby church was dedicated to the same saint. In 1948 it became part of the NHS and was amalgamated with the Royal Surrey County Hospital. In 1980 a new hospital was opened at Park Barn, retaining the name of the Royal Surrey County Hospital. However, the old building continued to be used; renamed Farnham Road Hospital, it specialised in catering for geriatric patients.

At the beginning of the 20th century the Surrey Archaeological Society had collected so many artefacts that in 1907 it persuaded the council that a museum was needed in which to house them. The council agreed, and Guildford Museum came into being. It was guaranteed a yearly income of £40, which was gradually raised to £100. In 1928 a muniment room was constructed in order to house manorial records from the surrounding area. Once this was established, there was a steady flow of documents into the museum, resulting in a much-needed civic archive. In 1933 the council took over responsibility for the museum, but the building still housed the Surrey Archaeological Society on its upper floors.

In 1947 the museum's first professional curator-archivist was appointed. The museum resisted all attempts to be a repository for a variety of unconnected objects: it was a local museum, and as such the curator decided that it should only illustrate the life of Guildford and its people. It has maintained its objective through the years, and still works closely with the Surrey Archaeological Society. It also welcomes schools to its doors. In the 21st century it has introduced pupils to life in a 'Victorian schoolroom': a room in the museum has taken on the role of 'a small village school near Guildford'. Children from local schools file in to take their places at the wooden desks and are taught by a Victorian schoolmistress. They have slates on which to write, discipline is strict and they learn by rote. What better way to learn about schools in the 19th century?

Billing's Printing Press continued to flourish during the 20th century, and in 1904 electricity replaced steam. The same year a machine shop and foundry encroached upon the garden at Coverdale. In 1900 Harrild, the eldest son, had become chairman of the company, and four years later his son, Bertram, was appointed secretary. In 1908 he was made a director. The firm had always been run on Christian principles and the Billings were always conscious of their responsibility to their employees, providing houses and flats for them. In 1913 one of the partners, Maurice Lacy, started a profit-sharing scheme, and in 1915 Robert Billing initiated a superannuation fund with a starting gift of £170. He started to write notes about the company, and during the First World War he

87   *Castle Arch, early 20th century.*   *Reproduced by permission of Surrey History Centre.*

88 *Town Mill, c.18th century.*

noted that 'every scrap of paper not then in daily use and also all file copies of books more than ten years old were sent away for pulping'. Not only therefore are records for the years 1900-19 non-existent, but many first editions which must have been of considerable value were also lost.[14] This was obviously a great loss, but it is hoped that the pulp was used to some effect for the war effort.

In 1914 Harrild died and the chairmanship passed to his brother, Robert. During his chairmanship a number of Bibles were printed in 'nearly 125 different languages and dialects' for the British and Foreign Bible Society, which had been established in 1804. Robert continued to work until 1928 when he officially retired, but he remained the chairman until 1936 when his nephew Bertram, Harrild's son, took over from him. Bertram continued in office until 1962, when an 'outsider', Alfred Owen, took over, and the Billings family no longer held a majority of the shares. Owen was enthusiastic, and oversaw extensive modernisation in all departments between the years 1963 and 1969.

The 1960s were difficult times for printers, and in 1964 Billings amalgamated with Unwins. Later it became a subsidiary of Blackwell Press. It continued for several years, but in March 1982 a decision was made to close the Guildford works after nearly 140 years.

EIGHT

The Cathedral and the University

Two important organisations were established in the second half of the 20th century: the cathedral and the university. The system of dividing the country into dioceses had been successfully used by the Church for over 1,000 years. In Whitby in A.D. 663 the Synod adopted the Roman rather than the Celtic way of worship. During the Roman empire a *propraetor* had been appointed to oversee a province that was not under military command; the Church continued the system, substituting a bishop for the *propraetor*. Over the centuries the bishops became powerful; they ruled over their domain not only as priests but also in a secular role.

Guildford was part of the vast diocese of Winchester, which originally stretched right across the south of England from Kent to Devon. During the 11th and 12th centuries it became smaller, incorporating only Hampshire and Surrey. It was not until the Reformation that any other changes took place, when Henry VIII appointed commissioners to look into the diocesan system. The population in the country had grown rapidly since the Middle Ages, and the commissioners recommended that five new dioceses should be created; they also decided that the bishop should be able to appoint an 'honest and discreet spiritual person' as a suffragan bishop to assist him. One of the areas in which a suffragan bishop could be appointed was Guildford. However, as the population of the town was still relatively small, this did not happen until 1874.

As the population continued to increase, in 1923 it was suggested that two new dioceses, Portsmouth and Guildford, should be created out of the large Winchester diocese. As was to be expected, there was great opposition to the idea, but in 1927 the new diocese of Guildford was created. In July of that year

89   *View of Cathedral from the north side.*

the Rev. Harold Greig was installed as the first Bishop of Guildford in Holy Trinity Church at the top of the High Street. This would become the new bishop's 'cathedral'. Although large, it was certainly not suitable for fulfilling all the functions that were traditionally performed in a cathedral.

Bishop Greig was determined that Guildford should have a cathedral of its own. It would be the first to be built in the south of England since the Middle Ages, but was it to follow the pattern of the earlier cathedrals or be a modern building? It would be an expensive project. Where was the money to come from? No longer were there wealthy patrons to provide funding. Church attendance had dropped during the 20th century, and many people were indifferent to the teachings of the Church.

In May 1928 a diocesan conference was held and, despite the obvious difficulties, the members took a step of faith and decided to erect a new cathedral. They were justified, as in November of the same year Richard, the 5th Earl of Onslow, gave a very welcome gift: six acres on the top of Stag Hill, an area unbuilt on and populated only by deer for centuries. He was willing to sell more of the land if it was required. This generous offer was accepted with alacrity, and a committee was formed to raise funds and supervise the eventual building. The estimated cost was £250,000. However, Lord Onslow stipulated that his offer should be taken up within three years.

The diocese was happy that they now had a definite site for the new building, but local residents were not so pleased. For one thing it was outside the town, and it was also suggested that the land might not be suitable for such a building: it would definitely need underpinning at great cost. Others objected to building on a site that had been a natural area of beauty for centuries. Why must man despoil nature? Many objected to the building of a cathedral at all. Fundraising would have to be mainly from the laity, and most people were facing great hardship. The Depression had set in after Wall Street had collapsed in November 1928, and the resulting chaos had forced thousands into unemployment across the United Kingdom. Guildford was no exception. Its residents had no money to spare for a cathedral that many of them did not even want. Even the Church itself was not happy about contributing vast amounts of money to a grandiose project when funds were urgently needed to build more parish churches.

But the diocese was not deterred, and was still 'desirous of erecting a cathedral'. In 1930 it announced a competition for architects to design a new cathedral, and 183 entries were received. At the end of January 1931 five finalists were selected; the final entries, consisting of detailed designs, were to be submitted by May 1932, and each finalist was paid a retainer of 500 guineas. The diocese was still not sure whether the design should be in the traditional Gothic style or a more modern structure. However, they eventually agreed that it 'should be in the line of the great English Cathedrals'.

On Saturday 23 July 1932 it was announced that Edward Marfe was the winner of the competition. He was delighted, feeling that the prominent site of Stag Hill was 'providentially made for a cathedral': the summit stood 259ft above sea level. He said:

> Above all else Guildford Cathedral should express the English spirit: it should be serene and grow naturally without effort out of Stag Hill itself ... The ideal has been to produce a design definitely of our time, yet in the line of the great English Cathedrals, to build anew on tradition, to rely on proportion of mass, volume and line rather than on elaboration and ornament.[1]

But there was still no money forthcoming, and the town showed no enthusiasm for the project. Then in 1931 the Mayor of Guildford, William Harvey, launched a successful appeal for funds to support those who had been made homeless as a result of the Depression. The following year Lord Middleton, the chairman of the Cathedral Appeal Committee, wrote to the mayor, who had great influence in the town, asking for his support. With regard to the siting of

90   *Erecting Teak Cross.*

the cathedral, he pointed out that that there were other cathedrals that were not central to the cities that they served. The mayor assured the forthcoming diocesan conference that, despite evidence to the contrary, Guildford *was* in favour of building a cathedral.

Although Harvey was vague in his response, it was decided to proceed. In December 1933, a dual appeal was launched, for building the cathedral and new parish churches. It was decided to begin work on the cathedral when £50,000 had been raised. To support this decision a large teak cross, made of timbers from the 19th-century battleship HMS *Ganges*, was erected on the summit of Stag Hill. It was unveiled in the spring of 1933 by Bishop Greig.

The money was slow coming in, but £36,000 had been raised by 1936. Although this was considerably less than the £50,000 that had been stipulated, it was decided that the building should commence immediately; the diocesan conference was confident that more money would be forthcoming once the work had started. The cathedral was to be dedicated to the Holy Spirit, the only cathedral in England to have such a dedication. This had been suggested by Bishop Greig, and was adopted in spite of various objections. Edward Maufe said that it had given him 'much trouble', but he was wholeheartedly in favour of 'this inspiring dedication'.

On 22 July 1936 about 10,000 people watched the Archbishop of Canterbury, Cosmo Gordon Lang, lay the foundation stone of the Cathedral of the Holy Spirit. It can be seen today behind the high altar. The building was to be constructed from bricks made from the very hill on which the cathedral was to stand.

Once started, work proceeded swiftly, and 778 piles were driven 50ft into the hillside on the west side of the teak cross. In 1937 Queen Mary was present as the last one was fixed in place. The clay that was removed to make room for the piles was used for making the bricks. The following year, on 25 May,

91   *Teak Cross in front of the Cathedral.*

the Mayor of Guildford, Harold Gammon, laid the first brick with a trowel engraved with the arms of the cathedral. By 1939 the choir had been completed, but still lacked a roof. Then disaster struck again. The Depression had halted the funding for the cathedral but now a world war prevented any building for several years. Fortunately a special licence was obtained so that a temporary roof could be put in place to protect the shell of the building. Even after the war, work could not be resumed immediately as so much housing was needed for those who had been bombed out of their homes. Completing a cathedral was very low down on the list of priorities. However, a permit was obtained so that the crypt could be furnished and consecrated. When this was finished, regular services were held in the crypt chapel. The nucleus of the cathedral congregation was being formed.

Finally, in 1952, a building permit was granted and work continued. Since its conception costs had risen dramatically, and the original estimate of £250,000 was now totally inadequate. Another fundraising drive was needed. Miss Eleanora Iredale, the secretary to the council, had an idea that proved very successful. She suggested that the public should be invited to buy a brick for half a crown – 2s. 6d. The 'buy a brick' fund-raising idea was taken up with enthusiasm, and both residents and those farther afield bought their 'piece of clay', knowing that they were contributing to a cathedral that, it was hoped, would stand high on the hill for centuries and be visible for miles around.

By 1954 the east end of the cathedral was almost completed, and a service attended by about 1,500 people was conducted by the new provost, Walter Boulton. In 1955 about 1,500 people took part in a diocesan pilgrimage to the new cathedral, where an open-air service was held. Princess Margaret attended, and a stone was set in the floor of the nave to commemorate her visit: 'This stone commemorates the visit of Her Royal Highness Princess Margaret on the 17th of April 1955 to mark the beginning of the building of the nave.' In June 1957, when the Queen and the Duke of Edinburgh visited Guildford to celebrate the 700th anniversary of the granting of the first charter to the town, they paid a visit to the cathedral. The nave was almost finished at this time, and another stone on the floor of the nave marks their visit: 'This stone commemorates the visit of Her Majesty Queen Elizabeth II and His Royal Highness the Duke of Edinburgh on the 27th June 1957 to mark the progress in the building of the nave.' During their visit they each bought a brick. These were not used in the building but, together with those bought by other members of the royal family, can be viewed today in the showcase in St Ursula's porch on the south side of the cathedral. There are five bricks signed with the following names: Philip, Margaret, Elizabeth R, Marina (Duchess of Kent) and Mary (Princess Royal).

92 *Pilgrimage to Cathedral site.*

93 *Pilgrims on horseback.*

94 *St Ursula.*

95 *The Queen arriving at the Cathedral in 1957.*

96 *The Queen signing a brick.*

97 *Princess Margaret arriving for the Pilgrimage.*

98 *The Queen chatting to clergy.*

The porch was given to the cathedral by Mr FitzSimon of Witley in memory of his wife Ursula – hence the name. St Ursula was the patron saint of schoolgirls and the statue of her, set in a niche on the east wall of the porch, was produced by the sculptor Vernon Hill. She is shown standing, with her right hand around the shoulders of a young girl while another child kneels at her feet. The sculptor created it in his London workshop during the Blitz. When it was completed he ferried it to the cathedral in a taxi. A few days later his workshop was completely destroyed in an air raid.

Meanwhile Holy Trinity Church was still enjoying its cathedral status, and the provost, Walter Boulton, berated both the town council and the citizens for their original lack of fervour. The mayor, Leslie Codd, supported his views. While having no interest in the Church, Codd felt that the building of a cathedral would add to the town's status. The brick appeal and the outspoken comments by influential men resulted in the raising of about £42,000, and work continued. By 1961 this figure had increased to £54,000, but £300,000 was still needed.

Although the work was not completed, the cathedral was suitable for use, so it was decided to fix a date for its consecration in May 1961. Sadly, Ivor Watkins, the Bishop of Guildford, had died in 1960, but a new bishop was hurriedly appointed and Holy Trinity Church hosted its last major event as a cathedral: on 12 April 1961 George Reindorp was enthroned there as the new Bishop of Guildford. Already there was controversy about the appointment of dean. As provost of the cathedral, as well as rector of Holy Trinity, Walter Boulton had confidently expected to resign his position as provost and be installed as dean. However, there was opposition to his appointment from influential quarters. When this became known many people were outraged, and a petition was sent to the queen supporting Boulton as dean. It never reached Her Majesty as it was diverted to the Prime Minister, who pointed out that the appointment of a dean had already been made and the queen had 'no ultimate responsibility' for appointments within the Church, although she had to agree the appointments of bishops.

Early in 1961, before the dedication of the cathedral, an organ, built by Rushworth & Dreaper Ltd, was installed. On 17 May that year, on a grey, overcast day, George Reindorp performed his first act as the fifth Bishop of Guildford, when he consecrated the new cathedral in the presence of Her Majesty the Queen. Present also were Edward Maufe, the proud architect, and Walter Boulton in his role as provost. He resigned, as expected, the following day. The new dean of the cathedral was George William Clarkson. In spite of having a cathedral, Guildford remains a borough. It can only become a city if it is granted a royal charter by the queen, and so far this has not happened.

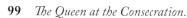

99   *The Queen at the Consecration.*

100   *The Queen signing the sentence of consecration.*

The fundraising continued, and over the following 40 years the sacristy, the lady chapel and the tower, with its ring of 10 bells, were finally completed. Below the steps leading up to the high altar a carpet designed by Sir Edward Maufe was laid. It was the last handmade carpet to be made at the famous Wilton factory. Two angels support the arms of the Diocese of Guildford; below them a stag reminds visitors of Stag Hill, where once stags reigned supreme and Norman kings hunted. On the floor in the centre of the nave the stag motif is repeated in an engraving. This marks the summit of Stag Hill, and also the centre of the cathedral. The design of each of the 1,460 handmade kneelers was approved by the architect's wife, Lady Maufe. Each has a unique pattern but all are divided diagonally. The blue lower half represents Stag Hill while the cream upper section represents the sky.

The total cost of the building was £900,000, considerably more than its original estimate. It was not until 2004 that Sir Edward Maufe's total design was completed. He had intended that the blocks of stone around the three west doors should be sculpted with statues, and his idea had not been forgotten. In 1999 a design competition for the statues was organised by the dean and chapter. The competition was won by the ecclesiastical sculptor Charles Gurney from York, who was commissioned to sculpt appropriate statues to fill the niches. He chose two women and six men whose lives reflected the Holy Spirit to whom the cathedral had been dedicated.

The first one was Lady Julian of Norwich, a 14th-century nun, who illustrated the importance of women in the Christian tradition. In contrast the lady next to her was from the early 20th century: Evelyn Underhill, an influential writer on prayer and the inner life of the Spirit. Still from the 20th century, Michael Ramsay was Archbishop of Canterbury from 1961 to 1974 and was an important figure in 20th-century Anglicanism; he even tried to forge links with the Roman Catholic Church. St Bernard of Clairvaux was a leader of the Cistercian monks in the 12th century; his beautiful hymns are still sung in churches today. Even further back in time was St Benedict, the sixth Abbot of Monte Cassino and the father of western monasticism. Returning to the 20th century, Reginald Somerset Ward was a priest in the Church of England who spent most of his life in Farncombe and advised people about their prayer life. Another figure from the same century was Bede Griffiths, regarded by some as one of the prophets of our age. Growing up in Walton-on-Thames, he became a Benedictine monk,

101　*Aerial view of Cathedral.*

Clockwise from top left:
102   *The stag on the floor of the nave in the centre of the Cathedral.*
103   *Lady Maufe.*
104   *Sir Edward Maufe and Bishop Macmillan.*

105   *Putting up the golden angel.*

but he was attracted to India and later lived for 30 years in the southern part of that country, where he encouraged greater understanding between East and West. The last figure was St Columba, the sixth-century Celtic abbot of Iona. The work on these statues was completed in April 2004.

Today Guildford Cathedral, with its golden angel on top, stands as a beacon overlooking the town. Floodlit at night, it can be seen from as far away as Heathrow. Sir Edward Maufe had originally envisaged an angel on top of his building, and in the 1960s William Pickford, a metalwork designer, was commissioned to design it. He worked closely with the architect who insisted that, while the face should be sexless, the fingernails and toenails should be carefully detailed. One wonders why, as they are impossible to see without the aid of binoculars! The angel cost £3,500, and was a gift to the dean and chapter from Mr and Mrs Adgey-Edgar in memory of their son, Reginald, who had died on active service during the Second World War on 5 January 1944. A service to consecrate the tower was held in May 1965.

On 3 April 2006 Guildford Cathedral was honoured to hold the annual service on Maundy Thursday, when the queen distributed Maundy money to a number of deserving pensioners. After the service she was entertained to lunch by the mayor in the Guildhall. Examples of the Maundy money are on show in the treasury, housed in a small area on the north side of the cathedral.

106   *Guildford Cathedral.*

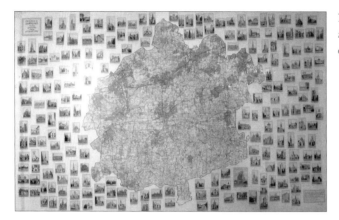

107   *John Clark's map of the Diocese of Guildford.*

Ian Pickford, an expert on English silver, officially opened the treasury on Wednesday 17 May 1995 after a choral evensong that celebrated the 34th anniversary of the consecration of the cathedral. The treasury provides a visible link between the cathedral and its parishes, preserving and caring for valuable objects that are no longer in use. Many of the objects on show belong to the cathedral itself: there are 215 parishes in the Diocese of Guildford but only 40 churches have lent artefacts; however, between them they have given about 150 items. The objects represent about 800 years of Church history, from the 12th to the 21st centuries, and they include a 12th-century bronze censer cover, a 16th-century 'Breeches' Bible, various communion cups and a 20th-century silver-gilt and enamel ceremonial key.

Near the treasury is a fascinating map created in 1954 by a 17-year-old schoolboy, John Clark. It shows a map of the Diocese of Guildford with photographs of every church placed on it in the appropriate places. Years later, after he retired, Mr Clark produced a larger map of the diocese. This time photos of the churches were placed around it, and the map now hangs on a wall in the treasury. It was dedicated in the year 2000 on Mothering Sunday.

In 1997 a garden of remembrance was dedicated; it sits opposite the teak cross at the east end of the cathedral and contains the ashes of former members of the cathedral congregation. Beside it is the Seeds of Hope garden. This was opened on Thursday 1 May 2008 by Dame Jacqueline Wilson, the children's author. In the centre of the garden is a beautiful sculpture of a boy and girl created by Christine Charlesworth. The plaque at the side describes it and explains the name of the garden: 'A girl makes dandelion seeds fly. A boy tries to catch them. All living things will die but their essence lives on in the new life that grows from the seeds of the old.' This is a garden for each of the four seasons, and in the winter garden is a small labyrinth marked out on the ground where the visitor can pause to meditate or perhaps walk around it. Continuing the remembrance theme, a small room on the north side of the cathedral has been dedicated as a memorial to children of all ages.

The cathedral did not expect the drama that unfolded on the afternoon of Sunday 30 November 2008 when David Sycamore, aged 39, appeared in the cathedral grounds waving a gun around. When the police received the call, they immediately went into action, and nearby residents heard the police helicopter hovering over the area for some time. A number of police tried to corner the man, who apparently suffered from depression. He had lived in Guildford all his life, and two years earlier he had told his parents 'he wanted to die in Guildford as he loved it so much'.[2] He had his wish on that fateful Sunday, as the police eventually shot him dead. It was later discovered that his gun was only a replica. His family was shocked and saddened by the event, and said that, in spite of his own depression, David had always tried to cheer up other people if they were sad. His mother described him as a 'lovely son'. The Dean of Guildford was concerned that the cathedral authorities had not been involved sooner, and felt that the police had not given 'enough consideration to the fact that Mr Sycamore was on sacred ground'.[3] However, he understood the pressure the officers were under, and that their main concern had been the safety of the public. An Advent carol service to which 500 people were expected was due to be held soon afterwards, but the police decided to cancel this – a decision the dean later questioned. Fortunately there have been no more untoward incidents of this kind.

2011 was the 50th anniversary of the consecration of the cathedral, and many events were planned throughout the year to celebrate the Golden Jubilee. One innovation at the beginning of the year was moving the small bookshop that had been located immediately outside the north door of the cathedral to the gift shop. The cathedral shop was officially opened by the dean, the Very Rev. Victor Stock, on Monday 10 January.

108   *Seeds of Hope Garden.*

109   *Font produced by Charley Gurney*
to celebrate the 50th anniversary.

The first major event to celebrate the anniversary was held in January; this was a drama workshops for schools entitled, appropriately, 'Bricks in the Wall'. This was arranged in partnership with Scenes Change. In February a service of hymns and popular anthems launched the year of celebration. In May there was even a Golden Jubilee Ball held in the nave of the cathedral. To celebrate the 50th anniversary the sculptor Charley Gurney created a portable altar and a new font, which now has pride of place in the nave. Another innovation was the loan of the Walking Madonna by the Woking Lightbox. This was created by Elizabeth Frink in 1981 and forms part of the Ingram Collection of Modern British Art. The year ended with a Golden Jubilee Christmas concert conducted by the composer John Rutter.

Today the cathedral is a hive of activity. Near the large car park there is now an education centre which is used for courses, lectures and school visits. Next to that is the refectory, which serves excellent food, and nearby is a gift shop. The cathedral itself plays host to exhibitions, concerts and dramas, and of course holds regular church services throughout the week. During the diocesan summer school held every July it hosts a variety of lectures and workshops. Others are held elsewhere in the diocese, including in other Guildford churches.

Next to the cathedral and its other buildings, still on the vast area known as Stag Hill, is the University of Surrey.[4] The idea of a university in Guildford had first been mooted in 1961, the year in which the cathedral had been consecrated. On 20 November that year the Guildford Rotary Club was addressed by the principal of the technical college. He praised the beneficial effects that the founding of a university could have on a town. Just three months later, on 1 January 1962, an electronics expert, Dr Robert Williams, addressed the same club and also referred to the effect on the town that the establishment of a new technological university could have.

For some time the governors of Battersea Technical College had felt that their 19th-century building could no longer cope with the 15,000 students who were currently enrolled. The college had been founded in 1891 as a charitable institution and admitted its first students in 1894. In 1956 it was one of the first colleges to be designated as a College of

110   *The Walking Madonna - on loan from the Lightbox*
(Ingram Collection of Modern British Art).

111 & 112 *University of Surrey.*

Advanced Technology; the following year it was renamed Battersea College of Advanced Technology. But it had outgrown its original building, and like many institutions founded in London in the 19th century it decided to seek a new facility away from the capital. What better place than Guildford, with its excellent rail services, good roads, a flourishing cultural tradition, a newly erected cathedral and beautiful countryside? An added attraction was the fact that the current principal knew Guildford well and was very impressed by its facilities.

Technology became increasingly important during the 1960s. In 1961 a committee to discuss the way forward for higher education had been convened under Lord Robbins. The seeds sown in the Guildford Rotary Club started to bear fruit, and a committee was formed to discuss the viability of the project. Would the citizens of Guildford support the idea of a university? If so, would the government approve an appropriate site? From the early planning stages there was no doubt that the prospective site was Stag Hill. Below the cathedral there was still a vast amount of land that could be utilised.

There was some local concern about the feasibility of housing such a vast number of students, but outweighing that was the fact that the building of a university would generate employment; the new 'residents' would spend money in the town and the university would become a high ratepayer. The latter may have been a contributory fact in the borough council giving its blessing to the idea in March 1963, although the project could not go ahead until it was given official recognition. Fortunately in October of the same year the Robbins Report was published, and its recommendations were accepted by the government on 24 October 1963. One of these was that colleges of advanced technology were to be given the status of universities.

Battersea College of Technology was designated as one of six new universities, but it was not until the following May that the idea born in the Rotary Club in 1961 became fact. The Secretary of State for Education and Science announced in the House of Commons that the University of Surrey was to be established in Guildford 'on a site to be provided from a fund to which both the governing body and the County Council will contribute'.[5] The site was, of course, Stag Hill and, as an academic organisation, it was appropriate the university should be next door to the cathedral: the Church and academia had worked closely together for centuries.

At first all did not go smoothly, and there were problems with the ownership of the land. The borough council was wholeheartedly in favour of the new university being built on Stag Hill; it owned the northern slope of the hill. and to show its support sold the land at considerably less than the market price. The use of this land had been limited to agricultural purposes but the restrictions were waived.

However, part of the area designated for building was Manor Farm, owned by the Onslow Village Association which was reluctant to sell. The villagers were particularly aggrieved because in 1954, when the village had applied for planning permission to build some houses on the land, their request had been refused. Now, apparently, 'foreigners' were to live in houses built on their land. They were not happy, and more protests followed. Eventually a compromise was reached: to sweeten the pill it was stressed that the land would be used for playing fields and not for building, so it would not be difficult to return it to its original agricultural purpose if the need arose. The village finally agreed to sell the land in March 1964. Had they not done so, a compulsory purchase order would have followed, no doubt.

But the protesters did not remain silent. There were a number of well-supported meetings at which great resentment was voiced over the speed in which the plans to build the university were being implemented, 'and the casual, haphazard manner in which the whole matter is being handled'.[6] The protests gathered momentum and eventually a public inquiry was held. While the minister was sympathetic to the objectors, he supported the building of the university, suggesting that it offered 'imaginative possibilities for the future of the town which only the most compelling objections could override'.[7]

Because of the protests, it was not until January 1966 that work on the site finally began. It was felt to be important that the university should integrate with the town, and the architects had a vision for 'a compact hill town ... not conceived as a military camp with fences and gatehouses but as an open, free, welcoming community, open to the town's people and nearer to the centre than any other postwar college or university'.[8]

At last, on 9 September 1966, the University of Surrey was granted its royal charter. The following month Lord Robens, chairman of the National Coal Board, was installed as its first chancellor in the new civic hall. Five honorary degrees were conferred on five eminent technologists and a sixth on Dame Sybil Thorndike, who had been involved in the foundation of the Yvonne Arnaud Theatre. The

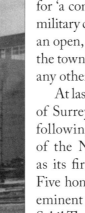

113 *Lord Robens, Chancellor of Surrey University.*

first Vice-Chancellor of the new university was to be the erstwhile Principal of the Battersea College of Advanced Technology; he paid tribute to the foresight of the Guildford Rotary Club, whose members comprised many professions and trades: 'If it had not been for the Guildford Rotary Club it is extremely unlikely that there would be a prospect of this university.'[9] The first graduation ceremony was held in the civic hall in 1970. In later years, if the civic hall was not available, the Odeon cinema was used. Eventually the cathedral became the venue for graduations.

Reminders of the original foundation of Battersea College of Technology were seen in the name of Battersea Court Hall of Residence. It was in June 1967 that the first students moved into their new university, negotiating their way over what was still virtually a building site. It was not until 1970 that the move from Battersea was finally completed. The estimated cost of establishing the university was £18,280,000 spread over 10 years. The bulk of this cost was to be covered by government grants, but £5,000,000 still needed to be raised. In May 1968 a fundraising appeal was launched.

The following January the borough council agreed to contribute £18,000 annually for 10 years. This was not popular with local ratepayers, who considered that the money should be spent on local facilities that needed repair and not on 'idle, unwashed students' who in the 1960s had an extremely bad press, because of the student riots both in Europe and the United Kingdom. However, the students from the new University of Surrey had not been involved. The National Union of Students stated that, 'at a time when students are rioting in Germany and France, and sitting outside the Vice-Chancellor's office of a British university, the name of Surrey University is missing from the headlines. This is because the Union effectively represents the student viewpoint to all levels of the University Administration ... primarily through the President who attends all meetings of Senate.'[10]

One day in April 1974 Ernest Shepard visited the university. A famous book illustrator, he is best known for his delightful illustrations of Winnie the Pooh. While not born in Guildford, he had a long association with the town; after his marriage he moved there, living there for 51 years. He had a purpose in visiting the university, and did not go empty-handed; with him he had a number of his drawings, manuscripts, diaries, papers and other memorabilia, which he presented to the Vice-Chancellor, feeling that their rightful place was in the archives of the local university. The archivist was delighted to receive them, and it was eventually decided that the unique and valuable collection should be given its own section in the university archive. Ernest Shepard died on 24 March 1976, two years after presenting his work. In his will he stipulated that no biography of him should be written until 30 years after his death.[11]

In 1982 the Guildford Institute in Ward Street acquired the University of Surrey as a trustee of its building. The university used this building for some of its adult courses, thus providing a university presence in the centre of Guildford. This arrangement continued until 2008, when the university ceased to be a trustee.

During the 1990s the university received several awards, including in 1991 the Queen's Award for Export Achievement, and in 1997 the Queen's Award for Higher and Further Education. The latter was given in recognition of its work in satellite engineering and communication.

The university has continued to flourish and develop in the 21st century. In 2002, to commemorate its 35th anniversary, it commissioned the sculptor Allan Sly to create an appropriate work that could be presented to the people of Guildford as an acknowledgement of the town's welcome to the university. He produced the Surrey Scholar, which was placed at the bottom of the High Street and shows a scholar cheerfully waving a mortar board towards the Downs. The sculpture was unveiled by the Duke of Kent on 29 May 2002, the plaque underneath it stating: 'This sculpture was presented to the Borough to celebrate Guildford as a place of culture and scholarship by Professor Patrick Dowling, Vice-Chancellor on behalf of the University of Surrey.'

In 2003 it was decided to allocate the Manor Park area as a site for residential accommodation for 683 students and 50 staff. Phase one was completed two years later. The promise not to build on this area had obviously been forgotten. Also in 2003 the university won the Queen's Anniversary Prize for Higher and Further Education for outstanding work by Professors Alf Adams and Brian Sealey and their research groups in the fields of ion beam applications and opto-electronics. The award ceremony took place at Buckingham Palace, and was attended by both professors and the Vice-Chancellor, Professor Patrick Dowling. The Surrey Sleep Research Centre was also launched that year,

114   *The Surrey Scholar.*

115   *Alan Turing statue.*

where sleep expertise from various disciplines was brought together.

Other accommodation was provided in 2004 when International House was opened to house 200 students. The same year the Minister of State for Lifelong Learning, Dr Kim Howells, opened the School of Management building. As well as housing computer laboratories and seminar rooms, there was a professional kitchen and restaurant suite. The university offered food degree programmes and students could demonstrate their hospitality and culinary skills in the restaurant, where the public were able to sample their excellent meals at a reduced cost. Opposite the new building His Royal Highness, the Earl of Wessex, unveiled a larger than life-size bronze statue of Alan Turing, who was widely renowned for his work with computers. He had once lived in Guildford.

In 2005 the Postgraduate Medical School was opened, and the following year saw the establishment of the Surrey International Study Centre in purpose-built accommodation. This catered for foreign students who wished to study selected courses at the university. A link was forged with the Dongbei University of Finance and Economics in China, which was given permission to award Surrey University degrees on its own campus.

In 1964 Bice Bellairs had founded the Guildford School of Acting and Dance and the university forged links with it. These were strengthened when the renamed Guildford School of Acting merged with the university, and in 2009 it relocated its premises to the Stag Hill campus. The university was proving that it provided cultural as well as technological facilities. Sport was not forgotten, and in 2010 Surrey Sport Park was opened in Manor Park.

NINE

The Twenty-first Century

Like the 20th century, the 21st century also started with floods; they were described as the worst since 1968. Rain fell continuously, and on 8 November 2000 the Wey once again burst its banks. Water seeped into the Yvonne Arnaud Theatre and the orchestra retreated to the wings as water filtered into the orchestra pit; four feet of water accumulated under the stage and the Mill studio next door could not be used for some time. Another theatre also suffered. The flood prevention doors at the Electric Theatre failed to stop water seeping in, and some archives were destroyed. The situation was so bad that for a time the police closed off all traffic to the town. Shoppers were affected when the basement of the Friary Shopping Centre was flooded with five feet of water. The ground floor of the newly refurbished Debenham's store was protected by a steel storm door, but the water was not to be defeated. It rose above it and seeped in through the ceiling.

Guildford continues to enjoy its reputation as a centre of culture, and with its cathedral high on the hill, a flourishing university, theatres, a variety of shopping areas and an excellent train service, it continues to attract both visitors and new residents. It has not forgotten its heritage, and many of its ancient sites have been restored and can be viewed by visitors. Its cobbled High Street is a reminder of the valuable work done by Henry Peak, and the statue of the Surrey Scholar at the end of the street brings the borough into the 21st century.

References

One   *Origins – The Anglo-Saxons*

1. Williamson, *Olden Time*, p.1
2. Matthew Alexander, p.14
3. *Ibid.*, pp.11-12
4. Williamson, *Olden Time*, p.42
5. *Ibid.*, p.43
6. The ends were thickened and curved back.
7. Russell, *Historical View*, p.99
8. E.R. Chamberlain, p.55
9. *Domesday*

Two   *The Normans and Medieval Guildford*

1. Robert Smith, Introduction to the *Official Guide of the 900th Anniversary Domesday*, 1986
2. Malden, p.292
3. Russell, *Historical View*, p.21
4. Manning and Bray, p.9
5. *Anniversary of the Domesday Book*
6. Manning and Bray, p.10
7. Brayley and Walford, p.102
8. Alexander, p.22
9. Malden
10. Manning and Bray, p.29
11. E.R. Chamberlain, p.80
12. Aubrey, vol. III, p.1718
13. Williams, *Olden Time*, p.45
14. Brayley and Walford, p.103
15. Guildford Museum website
16. Sandale's Register, Hants Record Society, pp.279-86

Three   *The Tudors and Stuarts*

1. Brayley and Walford, pp.20-1
2. E.R. Chamberlain, p.80
3. *Ibid.*, p.72
4. Williamson, *Olden Time*, p.65
5. *Ibid.*, p.55
6. *Ibid.*, p.2
7. Malden, p.115
8. *Ibid.*
9. *Ibid.*, p.116
10. *Ibid.*, p.378
11. Manning and Bray, p.32
12. Williamson, *Guildhall*, p.23
13. *Ibid.*, p.7
14. *Ibid.*, p.4
15. *Ibid.*
16. *Ibid.*, p.65
17. Matthew Alexander, p.30
18. Laurence
19. Williamson, *Guildford in the Olden Times*, p.43
20. *Ibid.*, p.90
21. Watson, p.9
22. *Ibid.*
23. *Ibid.*, p.11
24. *Ibid.*, p.12
25. Williamson, *Guildhall*, p.93
26. Watson, p.14
27. Malden, pp.6-7
28. Manning and Bray, vol. 1, p.4
29. Williamson, *Guildhall*, p.115

Four   *The Eighteenth Century*

1. http://en.wikipedia.org/wiki/ christopher_slaughterford
2. Manning and Bray, p.48
3. E.R. Chamberlain, pp.86
4. Matthew Alexander, pp.35-6
5. Bradley and Walford, p.187
6. http://en.wikipedia.org/wike/john_ russell
7. http://en.wikipedia.org/wiki/james_ price

Five   *The Nineteenth Century*

1. Morgan, pp.40-3
2. *Ibid.*, p.40
3. Williamson, *Guildhall*, p.184
4. Minutes of the Board of Guildford Guardians 1836-8
5. www.nationalarchives.gov.uk
6. www.nationalarchives.gov.uk
7. Oakley, p.27
8. Orwell, *Down and Out*, pp.154-5
9. *Ibid.*, pp.156-7
10. Alexander, p.115
11. Chamberlain, 149; Williamson, *Guildhall*, 165
12. Railway Minutes, p.1
13. Matthew Alexander, p.40

Six   *The Nineteenth Century Continued*

1. Billings, pp.6-7
2. Mason, p.60
3. *Surrey Advertiser*, 30 April 1864
4. Williamson, *Olden Time*, p 20
5. Russell, *Stranger's Guide*, p.3
6. *Ibid.*, p.49.
7. *Handbook*, p.139
8. E.R. Chamberlain, p.14
9. *Ibid.*, p.16; Peak, f.4410
10. Hooke, p.82
11. Peak, *Diaries*, p.6
12. *Ibid.*, pp.40-1
13. *Ibid.*, pp.125-6
14. *Ibid.*, p.133
15. E.R. Chamberlain, p.154; Peak, A, p.2
16. Peak, p.82
17. Peak, C, p.248

18. Peak, G, p.565
19. Morgan, p.3
20. Peak, D, pp.273-80
21. Morgan, p.36
22. *Ibid.*, p.93
23. *Ibid.*, p.97
24. *Ibid.*, p.104
25. *Ibid.*, p.105
26. *Ibid.*, p.106
27. *Ibid.*, p.100
28. *Ibid.*, p.115
29. *Ibid.*, p.118
30. *Ibid.*, p.120
31. Mary Alexander, *Lewis Carroll*

Seven   *The Twentieth Century*

1. *Official Guide to Guildford*, p.93
2. *Official Guide of the Chamber of Trade*, pp.12-13.
3. Oakley, p.10
4. *Ibid.*, p.17
5. *Ibid.*, p.27
6. *Ibid.*, p.28
7. *Ibid.*, p.75
8. *Ibid.*, p.170
9. *Ibid.*, p.142
10. *Ibid.*, pp.149-51
11. *Ibid.*, pp.197
12. *Ibid.*, pp.198
13. *Surrey Advertiser and County Times*, 29 June 1957
14. Billings, p.5

Eight   *The Cathedral and the University*

1. Maufe
2. *Surrey Advertiser*, 4 December 2008
3. *Ibid.*
4. *Ibid.*
5. *The Times*, 16 May 1964
6. *Surrey Advertiser*, 7 November 1964
7. *Ibid.*, 3 April 1967
8. *Guildford and Godalming Times*, 8 January 1966
9. E.R. Chamberlain, p.137
10. *Ibid.*, p.141
11. Chandler, p.9

Bibliography

Alexander, Mary, *Lewis Carroll and Guildford* (2010)

Alexander, Matthew, *Guildford – A Short History* (1986)

Aubrey, John, *The Natural History and Antiquities of the County of Surrey*

'Billings & Sons, Printers of Guildford', Surrey History Centre (ref. no. 1366).

Brayley and Walford, *Topographical History of Surrey*, vol. 1 (1848)

Chamberlain, E.R., *Guildford* (Phillimore and Co. Ltd, 1970/1982).

Chamberlain, Russell, *A History and Celebration of Guildford* (Frith Book Company, 2004)

Chandler, Arthur R., *The Story of E.H. Shepard – The Man who Drew Pooh* (Jaydem Books, 2000)

Domesday: Official publication of the National Domesday Committee for the 900th Anniversary of the Domesday Book (1986)

Encyclopedia Britannica

Guildford Today: the Official Guide of the Chamber of Trade, 1912

Guide: The Official Guide of the Corporation of Guildford (no date)

Hooke, *Guide to Guildford* (1894)

Manning, Owen and Bray, William, *The History and Antiquities of the County of Surrey*, vol. 1 (1804)

Malden, *Victoria County History of Surrey*, vol. 2 (1902)

Mason, J., *Guildford* (1897)

Maufe, Edward, *Architect* (Guildford Cathedral, 1971)

Minutes of the Reading, Guildford and Reigate Railway Company (no date)

Morgan, Gavin, *The Guildford Guy Riots* (Northside Books, 1992)

Oakley, W.H., *Guildford in the Great War: the Record of a Surrey Town* (Billings & Sons Ltd, 1934)

Orwell, George, *Down and Out in Paris and London* (Victor Gollancz, 1933)

Peak Diaries, Surrey History Centre

Russell, G.W and Russell, J.
   A Descriptive and Historical View of the County Town of Surrey (Longman and Co., 1845)
   Stranger's Guide to the Principal Objects of Interest in Guildford (1846)

Stend, W.A., *Handbook to Guildford* (1859)

Taylor, Brian, *Abbot's Hospital, Guildford* (St Thomas Trust, 1999)

Watson, Nigel, *The Royal Grammar School Guildford, An Illustrated History* (James & James (Publishers) Ltd, 2004)

Williamson, G.C.
   Guildford in the Olden Time (George Bell & Sons, 1904)
   The Guildhall of Guildford and its Treasures (Biddles Ltd, 1928)

Index

Castle grounds with bowling green and war memorial.